HOT & SPICY
COOKBOOK

HOT & SPICY
COOKBOOK

FIERY DISHES TO SPICE UP
YOUR KITCHEN

Consultant Editor: Linda Fraser

HERMES
HOUSE

First published in 1999 by Hermes House

© Anness Publishing Limited 1999

Hermes House is an imprint of Anness Publishing Limited
Hermes House, 88–89 Blackfriars Road
London SE1 8HA

This edition first published in 1999 in the Necessities™ imprint by
The Warehouse Ltd., 26 The Warehouse Way
Northcote, Auckland, New Zealand

ISBN 1 84038 225 2

A CIP catalogue record for this book is available from the British Library

Publisher: Joanna Lorenz
Senior Cookery Editor: Linda Fraser
Project Editors: Anne Hildyard, Linda Doeser
Designer: Siân Keogh
Illustrations: Madeleine David
Front cover: Lisa Tai, Designer; Thomas Odulate, Photographer;
Helen Trent, Stylist; Lucy McKelvie, Home Economist

Previously published as part of a larger compendium, *The Ultimate Hot and Spicy Cookbook*

Printed in Hong Kong/China

1 3 5 7 9 10 8 6 4 2

The publishers would like to thank the following people:
Recipes: Kit Chan, Jacqueline Clark, Roz Denny, Joanna Farrow,
Rafi Fernandez, Christine France, Silvana Franco, Sarah Gates, Deh-Ta Hsiung, Shehzad
Husain, Elizabeth Ortiz Lambert, Sallie Morris, Hilaire Walden,
Laura Washburn, Pamela Westland, Steven Wheeler, Judy Williams.
Photography: William Adams-Lingwood, Karl Adamson, Edward Allwright, David
Armstrong, Steve Baxter, James Duncan, Nelson Hargreaves,
Amanda Heywood, Janine Hosegood, David Jordan, Patrick McLeavey,
Michael Michaels, Thomas Odulate.
Food for Photography: Carla Capalbo, Kit Chan, Jacqueline Clark,
Joanne Craig, Rosamund Grant, Carole Handslip, Jane Hartshorn,
Wendy Lee, Lucy McKelvie, Annie Nichols, Jane Stevenson, Steven Wheeler, Elizabeth
Wolf-Cohen
Stylists: Hilary Guy, Clare Hunt, Maria Kelly, Patrick McLeavey, Blake Minton, Thomas
Odulate, Kirsty Rawlings.

NOTES
For all recipes, quantities are given in both metric and imperial measures and, where
appropriate, in standard cups and spoons. Follow one set, but not a
mixture, because they are not interchangeable.
Standard spoon and cup measurements are level.
1 tsp = 5ml, 1 tbsp = 15 ml; 1 cup = 250ml/8fl oz
Australian standard tablespoons are 20ml. Australian readers should use 3 tsp in place of 1
tbsp for measuring small quantities of gelatine, cornflour, salt, etc.
Medium eggs should be used unless specified otherwise

CONTENTS

INTRODUCTION

Variety may or may not be the spice of life – but spice is certainly what gives food its variety. From the sun-drenched Caribbean to the deserts of the Middle East, the dense jungles of Vietnam and Indonesia, the bustling pavement stalls of Thailand, the great plains of Africa, the crowded streets of Mexico and the spirited South-western United States, "hot and spicy" defines good eating for millions of people who would not dream of consuming bland, unseasoned food when they have the option of something livelier and much more exciting.

∾

The recipes in this book are divided into five sizzling chapters: Soups, Starters & Snacks, Fish & Seafood, Meat & Poultry, Vegetable & Vegetarian Dishes and Relishes. Familiar favourites include Mulligatawny Soup, Samosas, Barbecued Jerk Chicken and Salsa Verde, and there are also some more unusual dishes to set the palate tingling. Why not wake up the taste buds with Chilli Crabs, Spatchcocked Devilled Poussins, Kenyan Mung Bean Stew or Chilli Bean Dip?

∾

A comprehensive introduction provides a world-tour of hot and spicy ingredients – from allspice to turmeric. Hints and tips throughout offer helpful suggestions and ideas for varying the recipes. All the recipes are easy to follow with step-by-step illustrations of the key stages and the finished dishes are photographed in colour.

∾

Take your courage and the *Hot & Spicy Cookbook* in hand and prepare the most exciting meals you have ever tasted.

HOT AND SPICY INGREDIENTS

ALLSPICE
Available whole or ground, allspice are small, dark brown berries similar in size to large peppercorns. They can be used in sweet or savoury dishes and have a flavour of nutmeg, cinnamon and clove, hence the name.

CARDAMOM
These pods are green, black and creamy beige, green being the most common. Whole pods are used in rice and meat dishes to add flavour and should not be eaten. Black seeds are used in desserts.

CHILLIES
Chillies are available from greengrocers and supermarkets. They are grown on a dwarf bush with small dense green leaves, white flowers and red or green finger shaped fruit. In general, the green chilli is less hot and has a rather earthy heat; the red is usually hotter and is often very fiery.

To prepare chillies, remove the cap from the stalk end and slit it from top to bottom with a small knife. Under running water, scoop out the seeds with the knife point. The fire comes from the seeds so leave them if you like food to be fiercely hot. Chillies contain volatile oil that can irritate the skin and

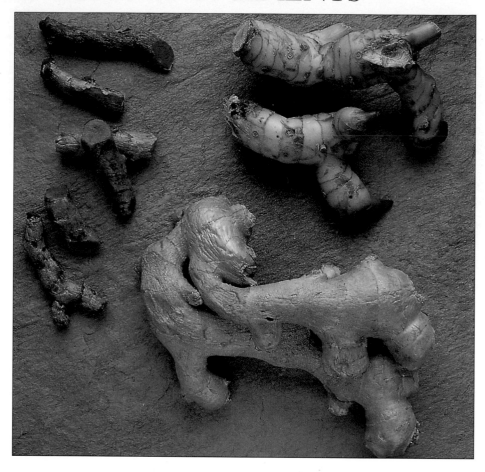

Clockwise from left: fresh turmeric roots before being ground to a fine powder, cut to show their vivid golden colour, creamy coloured fresh galangal roots, showing typical rings on the skin and pink nodules, and a large piece of unpeeled fresh ginger root showing the characteristic silvery brown skin.

From left: fresh, glossy lime leaves, lemon grass and fresh coriander leaves and root.

sting the eyes, so it is best to use rubber gloves when preparing chillies, or wash hands afterwards with soap and water.

There are many different varieties of chillies. The small red and green fresh chillies are known as Thai or bird's eye chillies and are extremely hot. One of the hottest varieties is the fat and fiery Scotch Bonnet or *habanero*. It has a spicy smell and flavour and can be red, green, yellow or brown. There are innumerable types of chillies that are indigenous to Mexico. The most commonly used fresh green chillies are *serrano*, *jalapeño* and *poblano*. These varieties are all very hot.

Dried chillies are very popular and

In the spice chest (top right), from the left: cayenne pepper, fennel seeds and ground turmeric. On the table: fresh red and green chillies. In the large bowl: a selection of ingredients for an Indian vegetarian curry: red chillies, aubergines, okra, bitter gourds, bay leaves, red peppers; and in the small bowl: dried coriander seeds.

there are numerous varieties available. The most commonly used dried chillies are *ancho*, which is full-flavoured and mild; *chipotle*, a very hot variety; *mulato*, which is pungent, and the hot *pasilla*.

CHILLI PRODUCTS

Cayenne pepper is a pungent spicy powder made from a blend of small ripe red chillies.

Chilli powder is made from dried, ground chillies and is often mixed with other spices and herbs.

Chilli flakes are made from dried, crushed chillies and are used in pickles and sauces.

Chilli oil is widely used in Chinese cooking. Dried red chillies are heated with vegetable oil to make this hot, pungent condiment.

Chilli paste is a convenient way of adding fiery heat to sauces.

Hot pepper sauce is made from red chillies and vinegar and is used to sprinkle over many dishes.

CINNAMON

Available as bark or in the ground form, cinnamon has a woody aroma with a fragrant and warm flavour. The powdered form is widely used in the Middle East, especially in Khoresh.

Clockwise from top left: red chillies, mild, glossy green Kenyan chillies, hot green chillies, green chillies, orange Thai chillies, red birdseye chillies and green birdseye chillies.

Cinnamon is a versatile spice and is good in lamb dishes as well as in spiced drinks, fruit compotes, chocolate cakes and desserts.

CLOVES

Cloves are used in spice mixtures such as garam masala and in many meat and rice dishes. They can also be used to add spicy flavour to fruit and desserts.

CORIANDER

This spice is used throughout the world. It is available as either whole seeds or ground powder. The ripe seeds have a sweet, spicy aroma with a hint of orange flavour. Coriander can be used in both sweet and savoury dishes and is one of the essential ingredients in curry powder. The flavour of coriander can be accentuated by dry-frying.

The leaves are essential in the cooking of South-East Asia and India and the root is often used in Thai cooking.

CUMIN

Cumin is available as small brown ridged seeds or in the ground form. Both types have a characteristic pungent, warm flavour. Cumin is also often dry-roasted to bring out the flavour. This spice is popular in the Middle East; it is used in spice mixtures such as garam masala and is added to pickles and salads. Cumin is one of the main ingredients of curry powder.

CURRY PASTE

Curry pastes are made by pounding spices with red or green chillies. They are ferociously hot and will keep for about 1 month in the fridge.

FISH SAUCE

Known as *nam pla,* this is a commonly used flavouring in Thai dishes in the same way that soy sauce is used in Chinese cooking. Fish sauce is made from salted anchovies and although not a spice, it contributes a depth of

Clockwise from top left: green jalapeño chillies, large green anaheim chillies, small green chillies, chipotle (smoked dried jalapeño chillies), dried mulato chillies, dried habanero chillies, dried pasilla chillies, green peppers, and (centre top left) yellow and red Scotch Bonnet chillies, (centre right) fresh red chillies.

pungent salty flavour to any dish.

FIVE-SPICE POWDER
This reddish brown powder is a combination of five ground spices – star anise seed, fennel, clove, cinnamon and Szechuan pepper. Used sparingly, it has a wonderful flavour, but it can be dominant if too much is added.

GALANGAL
This is a member of the ginger family and looks rather similar to fresh root ginger. The root is creamy coloured, with a translucent skin that has rings, and may have pink nodules rather like young ginger. It has a refreshing sharp, lemony taste and is best used fresh, although it is available in dried or powder form. If you cannot find fresh galangal, use about 5ml/1tsp of the dried powder to replace each 2.5cm/1in fresh galangal.

To prepare, cut a piece of the required size. Trim off any knobbly bits, then peel carefully, as the tough skin has an unpleasant taste. Slice to use in a paste and use up as soon as possible after peeling, to prevent loss of flavour. The flesh is much more woody and fibrous than ginger and has a distinctive, pine-like smell. Store galangal wrapped, in the salad drawer of the fridge.

GARAM MASALA
This spice mixture is made from a variety of spices and can be a simple blend, consisting of two or three spices

and herbs, or a more complex masala, made from twelve or more different spices. The dry spices and seeds are often dry-roasted first and sometimes whole spices are used. Indian cooks have their own individual recipes, but a typical mixture might include black cumin seeds, peppercorns, cloves, cinnamon and cardamom pods. Ready-made garam masala is available from most supermarkets and from Indian foodstores. Garam masala may be added to the dish at different cooking stages, usually towards the end of the total cooking time.

GINGER

A root of Chinese and Indian origin with a silvery brown skin, ginger is best used fresh, and should be peeled and chopped, grated or crushed before cooking. It is available from supermarkets – look for shiny smooth fat roots. Store, wrapped in kitchen paper, in the salad drawer of the refrigerator. Ginger is a good alternative to galangal in Thai cooking.

LEMON GRASS

This tropical grass has a fresh, highly aromatic lemony taste and is an essential ingredient in South-east Asian cooking. It combines well with garlic and chillies and is usually pounded to a paste before being added to curries. Unless it has been pounded or very finely chopped, lemon grass is usually removed before serving, as it has a very fibrous texture.

LIME LEAVES

These glossy, dark green, figure-of-eight-shaped leaves come from the kaffir lime tree. They have a pleasing, distinctive smell and can be torn into small pieces or left whole. Lime leaves can be frozen and used straight from the freezer in curries and sauces.

MACE AND NUTMEG

Mace and nutmeg are different parts of the fruit of the nutmeg tree. The fruit,

which is about the size of an apricot, splits to reveal brilliant red arils encasing the brown nut. The arils are the mace, and inside the nut is the nutmeg. Both parts of the fruit are dried before use. Nutmeg, which has a sweet, nutty flavour, is widely used all over the world. Whole nutmegs can be freshly grated for cooking or bought ready-ground, and are used in both savoury and sweet dishes. Mace is sold either as whole blades or ground, and is used in savoury dishes.

PAPRIKA

This is made from a mixture of ground dried red peppers. Both mild and hot peppers are used, but paprika is always milder than cayenne pepper or chilli powder. Sweet paprika is milder than hot paprika; always check the label. It is widely used in the Middle East in soups, meat dishes, salad dressings and as a garnish.

PEPPERCORNS

White, green and black peppercorns are berries from the same plant, picked at different stages of maturity, the black ones being the fully ripe berries. Pepper has a pungent flavour and can be used in either savoury or sweet dishes. Peppercorns can be used whole, crushed or ground.

SAFFRON

Made from the dried stamens of a type of crocus, saffron has a superb aroma and flavour. It also adds a delicate yellow colour to food. For the best results it should be ground to a powder and diluted in a small amount of boiling water.

SUMAC

The seeds of the Mediterranean sumac are widely used in Turkish and Middle Eastern cooking. They have a sharp fruity taste. The juice may be extracted for marinades and salad dressings. Ground sumac is used as a seasoning for grilled meat and fish stews.

SZECHUAN PEPPER

Szechuan pepper is also known as anise pepper. The berries are red-brown in colour and are prickly. They are spicy with a rather numbing taste. They provide the characteristic flavour of Szechuan cuisine.

TAMARIND

An acidic-tasting tropical fruit that resembles a bean pod, it is added to curries to give a sharp flavour. Tamarind is usually sold dried or pulped. To make tamarind juice, soak a piece of tamarind pulp in warm water for about ten minutes. Squeeze out as much tamarind juice as possible by pressing all the liquid through a strainer with the back of a spoon.

TURMERIC

Turmeric is another member of the ginger family. When the whole spice is peeled or scraped, a rich golden root is revealed. Turmeric adds a distinctive flavour and rich yellow colour to meat and rice dishes. It is widely used throughout the Middle East and India. Because of its strong, bitter flavour, turmeric should be used sparingly. Protect your hands from staining if you are using the raw root.

Opposite page: A selection of spices, from left to right from the top row: paprika, whole green cardamoms, cumin seeds, saffron strands, ground turmeric, whole nutmeg and mace, ground sumac, cinnamon sticks and ground nutmeg.

SOUPS, STARTERS & SNACKS

Tamarind Soup with Peanuts and Vegetables

Sayur Asam is a colourful and refreshing soup from Jakarta with more than a hint of sharpness.

INGREDIENTS

Serves 4 or 8 as part of a buffet
For the spice paste
5 shallots or 1 medium red
    onion, sliced
3 garlic cloves, crushed
2.5cm/1in *lengkuas*, peeled and sliced
1–2 fresh red chillies, seeded and sliced
25g/1oz raw peanuts
1cm/½in cube *terasi*, prepared
1.2 litres/2 pints/5 cups well-
    flavoured stock
50–75g/2–3oz salted peanuts,
    lightly crushed
15–30ml/1–2 tbsp dark brown sugar
5ml/1 tsp tamarind pulp, soaked in
    75ml/5 tbsp warm water for
    15 minutes
salt

For the vegetables
1 chayote, thinly peeled, seeds
    removed, flesh finely sliced
115g/4oz French beans, trimmed and
    finely sliced
50g/2oz sweetcorn kernels (optional)
handful green leaves, such as
    watercress, rocket or Chinese leaves,
    finely shredded
1 fresh green chilli, sliced, to garnish

1 Prepare the spice paste by grinding the shallots or onion, garlic, *lengkuas*, chillies, raw peanuts and *terasi* to a paste in a food processor or with a pestle and mortar.

2 Pour in some of the stock to moisten and then pour this mixture into a pan or wok, adding the rest of the stock. Cook for 15 minutes with the lightly crushed peanuts and sugar.

3 Strain the tamarind, discarding the seeds, and reserve the juice.

4 About 5 minutes before serving, add the chayote slices, beans and sweetcorn, if using, to the soup and cook fairly rapidly. At the last minute, add the green leaves and salt to taste.

5 Add the tamarind juice and taste for seasoning. Serve, garnished with slices of green chilli.

Pumpkin and Chilli Soup

INGREDIENTS

Serves 4–6

2 garlic cloves, crushed
4 shallots, finely chopped
2.5ml/½ tsp shrimp paste
15ml/1 tbsp dried shrimps soaked for
   10 minutes and drained
1 stalk lemon grass, chopped
2 green chillies, seeded
salt, to taste
600ml/1 pint/2½ cups chicken stock
450g/1lb pumpkin, cut into 2cm/¾in
   thick chunks
600ml/1 pint/2½ cups coconut cream
30ml/2 tbsp fish sauce
5ml/1 tsp granulated sugar
115g/4oz small cooked shelled prawns
freshly ground black pepper
2 red chillies, seeded and finely sliced,
   to garnish
10–12 basil leaves, to garnish

1 Grind the garlic, shallots, shrimp paste, dried shrimps, lemon grass, green chillies and salt into a paste.

2 In a large saucepan, bring the chicken stock to the boil, add the ground paste and stir to dissolve.

3 Add the pumpkin and simmer for about 10–15 minutes or until the pumpkin is tender.

4 Stir in the coconut cream, then bring back to a simmer. Add the fish sauce, sugar and ground black pepper to taste.

5 Add the prawns and cook until they are heated through. Serve garnished with the sliced red chillies and basil leaves.

--- COOK'S TIP ---

Shrimp paste, which is made from ground shrimps fermented in brine, is used to give food a savoury flavour.

Spicy Vegetable Soup

INGREDIENTS

Serves 4

½ red onion
175g/6oz each, turnip, sweet potato
    and pumpkin
30ml/2 tbsp butter or margarine
5ml/1 tsp dried marjoram
2.5ml/½ tsp ground ginger
1.5ml/¼ tsp ground cinnamon
15ml/1 tbsp chopped spring onion
1 litre/1¾ pint/4 cups well-flavoured
    vegetable stock
30ml/2 tbsp flaked almonds
1 fresh chilli, seeded and chopped
5ml/1 tsp sugar
25g/1oz creamed coconut
salt and freshly ground black pepper
chopped coriander, to garnish

1 Finely chop the onion, then peel the turnip, sweet potato and pumpkin and chop into medium-size dice.

2 Melt the butter or margarine in a large non-stick saucepan. Fry the onion for 4–5 minutes. Add the diced vegetables and fry for 3–4 minutes.

3 Add the marjoram, ginger, cinnamon, spring onion, salt and pepper. Fry over a low heat for about 10 minutes, stirring frequently.

4 Add the vegetable stock, flaked almonds, chopped chilli and sugar and stir well to mix, then cover and simmer gently for 10–15 minutes until the vegetables are just tender.

5 Grate the creamed coconut into the soup and stir to mix. Sprinkle with chopped coriander, if liked, spoon into warmed bowls and serve.

Spiced Lamb Soup

INGREDIENTS

Serves 4

115g/4oz split black-eyed beans,
  soaked for 1–2 hours, or overnight
675g/1½lb neck of lamb, cut into
  medium-size chunks
5ml/1 tsp chopped fresh thyme, or
  2.5ml/½ tsp dried
2 bay leaves
1.2 litres/2 pints/5 cups stock or water
1 onion, sliced
225g/8oz pumpkin, diced
2 black cardamom pods
7.5ml/1½ tsp ground turmeric
15ml/1 tbsp chopped fresh coriander
2.5ml/½ tsp caraway seeds
1 fresh green chilli, seeded and chopped
2 green bananas
1 carrot
salt and freshly ground black pepper

1 Drain the black-eyed beans, place them in a saucepan and cover with fresh cold water.

2 Bring the beans to the boil, boil rapidly for 10 minutes and then reduce the heat and simmer, covered for 40–50 minutes until tender, adding more water if necessary. Remove from the heat and set aside to cool.

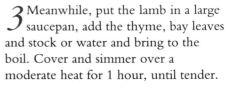

3 Meanwhile, put the lamb in a large saucepan, add the thyme, bay leaves and stock or water and bring to the boil. Cover and simmer over a moderate heat for 1 hour, until tender.

4 Add the onion, pumpkin, cardamoms, turmeric, coriander, caraway, chilli and seasoning and stir. Bring back to a simmer and then cook, uncovered, for 15 minutes until the pumpkin is tender, stirring occasionally.

5 When the beans are cool, spoon into a blender or food processor with their liquid and blend to a smooth purée.

6 Cut the bananas into medium slices and the carrot into thin slices. Stir into the soup with the beans and cook for 10–12 minutes, until the vegetables are tender. Adjust seasoning and serve.

Mulligatawny Soup

Mulligatawny (which means "pepper water") was introduced into England in the late eighteenth century by members of the army and colonial service returning home from India.

INGREDIENTS

Serves 4

50g/2oz/4 tbsp butter or
  60ml/4 tbsp oil
2 large chicken joints, about
  350g/12oz each
1 onion, chopped
1 carrot, chopped
1 small turnip, chopped
about 15ml/1 tbsp curry powder,
  to taste
4 cloves
6 black peppercorns, lightly crushed
50g/2oz/¼ cup lentils
900ml/1½ pints/3¾ cups
  chicken stock
40g/1½oz/¼ cup sultanas
salt and ground black pepper

1 Melt the butter or heat the oil in a large saucepan, then brown the chicken over a brisk heat. Transfer the chicken to a plate.

2 Add the chopped onion, carrot and turnip to the saucepan and cook, stirring occasionally, until they are lightly coloured. Stir in the curry powder, cloves and black peppercorns and cook for 1–2 minutes more before adding the lentils.

3 Pour the stock into the pan, bring to the boil, then add the sultanas and chicken and any juices from the plate. Cover and simmer gently for about 1¼ hours.

4 Remove the chicken from the pan and discard the skin and bones. Chop the flesh, return to the soup and reheat. Check the seasoning before serving the soup piping hot.

COOK'S TIP

Choose red split lentils for the best colour, although either green or brown lentils could also be used.

Plantain Soup with Corn and Chilli

INGREDIENTS

Serves 4

25g/1oz/2 tbsp butter or margarine
1 onion, finely chopped
1 garlic clove, crushed
275g/10oz yellow plantains, peeled and sliced
1 large tomato, peeled and chopped
175g/6oz/1 cup sweetcorn
5ml/1 tsp dried tarragon, crushed
900ml/1½ pints/3¾ cups vegetable or chicken stock
1 green chilli, seeded and chopped
pinch of grated nutmeg
salt and freshly ground black pepper

1 Melt the butter or margarine in a saucepan over a moderate heat, add the onion and garlic and fry for a few minutes until the onion is soft.

2 Add the plantain, tomato and sweetcorn and cook for 5 minutes.

3 Add the tarragon, vegetable stock, chilli and salt and pepper and simmer for 10 minutes or until the plantain is tender. Stir in the nutmeg and serve at once.

Spicy Groundnut Soup

This soup is widely eaten in Africa. Groundnuts (or peanuts) are spiced with a mixture of fresh ginger and chilli powder with herbs added for extra flavour. The amount of chilli powder can be varied according to taste, add more for a fiery hot soup.

INGREDIENTS

Serves 4

45ml/3 tbsp pure groundnut paste or peanut butter
1.5 litres/2½ pints/6¼ cups stock or water
30ml/2 tbsp tomato purée
1 onion, chopped
2 slices fresh root ginger
1.5ml/¼ tsp dried thyme
1 bay leaf
salt and chilli powder
225g/8oz white yam, diced
10 small okras, trimmed (optional)

1 Place the groundnut paste or peanut butter in a bowl, add 300ml/½ pint/1¼ cups of the stock or water and the tomato purée and blend together to make a smooth paste.

2 Spoon the nut mixture into a saucepan and add the onion, ginger, thyme, bay leaf, salt, chilli and the remaining stock.

3 Heat gently until simmering, then cook for 1 hour, stirring from time to time to prevent the nut mixture sticking.

4 Add the white yam, cook for a further 10 minutes, and then add the okra, if using, and simmer until both are tender. Serve at once.

Butterflied Prawns in Chilli Chocolate

Although the combination of hot and sweet flavours may seem odd, this is a delicious starter. The use of bitter chocolate adds richness without increasing the sweetness.

INGREDIENTS

Serves 4

8 large raw prawns, in the shell
15ml/1 tbsp seasoned flour
15ml/1 tbsp dry sherry
juice of 4 clementines or 1 large orange
15g/½oz unsweetened dark chocolate, chopped
30ml/2 tbsp olive oil
2 garlic cloves, finely chopped
2.5cm/1in piece fresh root ginger, finely chopped
1 small red chilli, seeded and chopped
salt and freshly ground black pepper

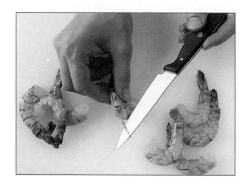

1 Peel the prawns, leaving just the tail sections intact. Make a shallow cut down the back of each prawn and carefully pull out and discard the dark intestinal tract. Turn over the prawns so that the undersides are uppermost, then carefully split them open from tail to top, using a small sharp knife, cutting almost, but not quite, through to the back.

2 Press the prawns down firmly to flatten them out. Coat with the seasoned flour and set aside.

3 Gently heat the sherry and clementine or orange juice in a small saucepan. When warm, remove from the heat and stir in the chopped chocolate until melted.

4 Heat the olive oil in a frying pan. Fry the garlic, ginger and chilli over a moderate heat for 2 minutes until golden. Remove with a slotted spoon and reserve. Add the prawns, cut-side down, to the pan; cook for 2–3 minutes until golden brown with pink edges. Turn and cook for a further 2 minutes.

5 Return the garlic mixture to the pan and pour over the chocolate sauce. Cook for 1 minute, turning the prawns to coat them in the glossy sauce. Season to taste and serve hot.

Spicy Potatoes

Spicy potatoes, *patatas picantes,* are among the most popular tapas dishes in Spain, where they are sometimes described as *patatas bravas* (wild potatoes). There are many variations of this classic: boiled new potatoes or large wedges of fried potato may be used, but they are perhaps best simply roasted as in this recipe.

INGREDIENTS

Serves 2 – 4
225g/8oz small new potatoes
15ml/1 tbsp olive oil
5ml/1 tsp paprika
5ml/1 tsp chilli powder
2.5ml/½ tsp ground cumin
2.5ml/½ tsp salt
flat leaf parsley, to garnish

1 Preheat the oven to 200°C/400°F/ Gas 6. Prick the skin of each potato in several places with a fork, then place them in a bowl.

2 Add the olive oil, paprika, chilli, cumin and salt and toss well.

3 Transfer the potatoes to a roasting tin and bake for 40 minutes.

--- COOK'S TIP ---

This dish is delicious served with tomato sauce or Fiery Salsa – provide small forks for dipping.

4 During cooking, remove the potatoes from the oven and turn occasionally, until tender. Serve hot, garnished with flat leaf parsley.

San Francisco Chicken Wings

INGREDIENTS

Serves 4

75ml/5 tbsp soy sauce
15ml/1 tbsp light brown sugar
15ml/1 tbsp rice vinegar
30ml/2 tbsp dry sherry
juice of 1 orange
5cm/2in strip of orange peel
1 star anise
5ml/1 tsp cornflour
50ml/2fl oz/¼ cup water
15ml/1 tbsp chopped fresh
   root ginger
5ml/1 tsp chilli-garlic sauce, to taste
1.5kg/3–3½lb chicken wings,
   tips removed

1 Preheat the oven to 200°C/400°F/ Gas 6. Mix the soy sauce, sugar, vinegar, sherry, orange juice and peel and anise in a pan. Bring to the boil.

2 Combine the cornflour and water in a small bowl and stir until blended. Add to the boiling soy sauce mixture, stirring well. Boil for another minute, stirring constantly.

3 Remove the soy sauce mixture from the heat and stir in the ginger and chilli-garlic sauce.

4 Arrange the chicken wings, in one layer, in a large baking dish. Pour over the soy sauce mixture and stir to coat the wings evenly.

5 Bake in the centre of the oven for 30–40 minutes until the chicken wings are tender and browned, basting occasionally. Serve the chicken wings either hot or warm.

Samosas

A selection of highly spiced vegetables in a pastry casing makes these samosas a delicious snack at any time of the day.

INGREDIENTS

Makes 30

1 packet spring roll pastry, thawed and
  wrapped in a damp towel
vegetable oil, for deep-frying

For the filling

3 large potatoes, boiled and
  coarsely mashed
75g/3oz/³/₄ cup frozen peas, thawed
50g/2oz/¹/₃ cup canned
  sweetcorn, drained
5ml/1 tsp ground coriander
5ml/1 tsp ground cumin
5ml/1 tsp amchur (dry mango powder)
1 small onion, finely chopped
2 green chillies, finely chopped
30ml/2 tbsp coriander leaves, chopped
30ml/2 tbsp mint leaves, chopped
juice of 1 lemon
salt, to taste
chilli sauce, to serve

1 Toss all the filling ingredients together in a large mixing bowl until they are all well blended. Adjust the seasoning with salt and lemon juice, if necessary.

2 Using one strip of pastry at a time, place 15ml/1 tbsp of the filling mixture at one end of the strip and diagonally fold the pastry up to form a triangle shape.

3 Heat enough oil for deep-frying and fry the samosas in small batches until they are golden brown. Keep them hot while frying the rest. Serve hot with chilli sauce.

Desert Nachos

Tortilla chips are livened up with jalapeños in this quick-and-easy snack. Served with a variety of spicy Mexican dips, this always proves to be a popular dish.

INGREDIENTS

Serves 2
450g/1lb blue corn tortilla chips or ordinary tortilla chips
45ml/3 tbsp chopped pickled jalapeños, according to taste
12 black olives, sliced
225g/8oz/2 cups grated Cheddar cheese

To serve
guacamole
tomato salsa
soured cream

1 Preheat the oven to 180°C/350°F/ Gas 4. Put the tortilla chips in a 23 x 33cm/9 x 13in baking dish and spread them out evenly. Sprinkle the jalapeños, olives and cheese evenly over the tortilla chips.

2 Place the prepared tortilla chips in the top of the oven and bake for 10–15 minutes until the cheese melts. Serve the nachos at once, with the guacamole, tomato salsa and soured cream for dipping.

Huevos Rancheros

INGREDIENTS

Serves 4
450g/1lb can refried beans
300ml/½ pint/1¼ cups enchilada sauce
oil, for frying
4 corn tortillas
4 eggs
150g/5oz/1¼ cups grated Cheddar cheese
salt and ground black pepper

1 Heat the refried beans in a saucepan. Cover and set aside.

2 Heat the enchilada sauce in a small saucepan. Cover and set aside.

3 Preheat the oven to 110°C/225°F/ Gas ¼. Put a 5mm/¼in layer of oil in a small non-stick frying pan and heat carefully. When the oil is hot, add the tortillas, one at a time, and fry for about 30 seconds on each side, until just crisp. Remove and drain the tortillas on kitchen paper and keep them warm on a baking sheet in the oven. Discard the oil used for frying. Let the pan cool slightly, then wipe it with kitchen paper to remove all but a film of oil.

4 Heat the frying pan over a low heat. Break in two eggs and cook until the whites are just set. Season with salt and pepper, then transfer to the oven to keep warm. Repeat to cook the remaining eggs.

5 To serve, place a tortilla on each of four plates. Spread a layer of refried beans over each tortilla, then top each with an egg. Spoon over the warm enchilada sauce, then sprinkle with the cheese. Serve hot.

COOK'S TIP

For a simple enchilada sauce, blend a can of tomatoes with 3 garlic cloves, 1 chopped onion, 45ml/3 tbsp chilli powder, 5ml/1 tsp each cayenne and cumin, and 2.5ml/½ tsp each dried oregano and salt.

Chillied Monkfish Parcels

Hot red chilli, garlic and lemon rind add tangy flavour to monkfish in these tasty little parcels.

INGREDIENTS

Serves 4

175g/6oz/1½ cups strong plain flour
2 eggs
115g/4oz skinless monkfish fillet, diced
grated rind of 1 lemon
1 garlic clove, chopped
1 small red chilli, seeded and sliced
45ml/3 tbsp chopped fresh parsley
30ml/2 tbsp single cream

For the tomato oil

2 tomatoes, peeled, seeded and
    finely diced
45ml/3 tbsp extra virgin olive oil
30ml/1 tbsp fresh lemon juice
salt and freshly ground black pepper

1 Place the flour, eggs and 2.5ml/½ tsp salt in a food processor; pulse until the mixture forms a soft dough. Knead for 2–3 minutes then wrap in clear film. Chill for 20 minutes.

2 Place the monkfish, lemon rind, garlic, chilli and parsley in the clean food processor; process until very finely chopped. Add the cream, with plenty of salt and pepper and whizz again to form a very thick purée.

3 Make the tomato oil by stirring the diced tomato with the olive oil and lemon juice in a bowl. Add salt to taste. Cover and chill.

4 Roll out the dough on a lightly floured surface and cut out 32 rounds, using a 4cm/1½in plain cutter. Divide the filling among half the rounds, then cover with the remaining rounds. Pinch the edges tightly to seal, trying to exclude as much air as possible.

5 Bring a large saucepan of water to simmering point and poach the parcels, in batches, for 2–3 minutes or until they rise to the surface. Drain and serve hot, drizzled with the tomato oil.

Devilled Kidneys

"Devilled" dishes are always hot and spicy. If you have time, mix the spicy ingredients together in advance to give the flavours time to mingle and mature.

INGREDIENTS

Serves 4
10ml/2 tsp Worcestershire sauce
15ml/1 tbsp prepared English mustard
15ml/1 tbsp lemon juice
15ml/1 tbsp tomato purée
pinch of cayenne pepper
40g/1½oz/3 tbsp butter
1 shallot, finely chopped
8 lamb's kidneys, skinned,
  halved and cored
salt and ground black pepper
15ml/1 tbsp chopped fresh parsley,
  to garnish

1 Mix the Worcestershire sauce, mustard, lemon juice, tomato purée, cayenne pepper and salt together to make a sauce.

2 Melt the butter in a frying pan, add the chopped shallot and cook, stirring occasionally, until it is softened but not coloured.

3 Stir the kidney halves into the shallot in the pan and cook over a medium-high heat for about 3 minutes on each side.

4 Pour the sauce over the kidneys and quickly stir so that they become evenly coated. Serve the dish immediately, sprinkled with fresh chopped parsley.

COOK'S TIP

To remove the cores from the lamb's kidneys, use sharp kitchen scissors, rather than a knife – you will find that it is much easier to do so.

FISH & SEAFOOD

Fried Catfish Fillets with Piquant Sauce

Spicy fillets of catfish are fried in a herby batter and served with a wonderfully tasty sauce to create this excellent supper dish.

INGREDIENTS

Serves 4
1 egg
50ml/2fl oz/¼ cup olive oil
squeeze of lemon juice
2.5ml/½ tsp chopped fresh dill
4 catfish fillets
50g/2oz/½ cup flour
25g/1oz/2 tbsp butter or margarine
salt and ground black pepper

For the sauce

1 egg yolk
30ml/2 tbsp Dijon mustard
30ml/2 tbsp white wine vinegar
10ml/2 tsp paprika
300ml/½ pint/1¼ cups olive or
   vegetable oil
30ml/2 tbsp prepared horseradish
2.5ml/½ tsp chopped garlic
1 celery stick, chopped
30ml/2 tbsp tomato ketchup
2.5ml/½ tsp ground black pepper
2.5ml/½ tsp salt

1 For the sauce, combine the egg yolk, mustard, vinegar and paprika in a mixing bowl. Add the oil in a thin stream, beating vigorously with a wire whisk to blend it in.

2 When the mixture is smooth and thick, beat in all the other sauce ingredients. Cover and chill until ready to serve.

3 Combine the egg, 15ml/1 tbsp olive oil, the lemon juice, dill and a little salt and pepper in a shallow dish. Beat until well combined.

4 Dip both sides of each catfish fillet in the egg and herb mixture, then coat lightly with flour, shaking off any excess from it.

5 Heat the butter or margarine with the remaining olive oil in a large heavy-based frying pan. Add the fish fillets and fry until they are golden brown on both sides and cooked, for about 8–10 minutes. To test they are done, insert the point of a sharp knife into the fish: the flesh should be opaque in the centre.

6 Serve the fried catfish fillets hot, accompanied by the piquant sauce in a dish.

COOK'S TIP

If you can't find catfish, use any firm fish fillets instead. Cod or haddock fillets would both make good substitutes.

Braised Fish in Chilli and Garlic Sauce

INGREDIENTS

Serves 4–6

1 bream or trout, 675g/1½lb, gutted
15ml/1 tbsp light soy sauce
15ml/1 tbsp Chinese rice wine
vegetable oil, for deep-frying

For the sauce

2 garlic cloves, finely chopped
2–3 spring onions, finely chopped
5ml/1 tsp chopped fresh root ginger
30ml/2 tbsp chilli bean sauce
15ml/1 tbsp tomato purée
10ml/2 tsp light brown sugar
15ml/1 tbsp rice vinegar
about 120ml/4fl oz/½ cup fish stock
15ml/1 tbsp cornflour paste
few drops sesame oil

1 Rinse and dry the fish well. Using a sharp knife, score both sides of the fish as far down as the bone with diagonal cuts about 2.5cm/1in apart. Rub the whole fish with soy sauce and wine on both sides, then leave to marinate for 10–15 minutes.

2 In a wok, deep-fry the fish in hot oil for about 3–4 minutes on both sides until golden brown.

3 Pour off the excess oil, leaving a thin layer in the wok. Push the fish to one side of the wok and add the garlic, the white part of the spring onions, fresh ginger, chilli bean sauce, tomato purée, brown sugar, rice vinegar and stock. Bring to the boil and braise the fish in the sauce for about 4–5 minutes, turning it over once. Add the green part of the chopped spring onions. Thicken the sauce with the cornflour paste, sprinkle with the sesame oil and place on a dish to serve immediately.

VARIATION

Any whole fish is suitable for this dish; try sea bass, grouper or grey mullet, if you like. Also, if you can't find Chinese wine, use dry sherry instead.

Turkish Cold Fish

Green chilli, garlic and paprika
add subtle spicing to this
delicious fish dish. Cold fish is
enjoyed in many parts of the
Middle East – this particular
version is from Turkey.

INGREDIENTS

Serves 4
60ml/4 tbsp olive oil
900g/2lb red mullet or snapper
2 onions, sliced
1 green chilli, seeded and chopped
1 each red and green pepper, sliced
3 garlic cloves, crushed
15ml/1 tbsp tomato purée
50ml/2fl oz/¼ cup fish stock
  or water
5–6 tomatoes, peeled and sliced or
  400g/14oz can tomatoes
30ml/2 tbsp chopped fresh parsley
30ml/2 tbsp lemon juice
5ml/1 tsp paprika
15–20 green and black olives
salt and freshly ground black pepper
bread and salad, to serve

1 Heat 30ml/2 tbsp of the oil in a
large roasting tin or frying pan and
fry the fish on both sides until golden
brown. Remove from the tin or pan,
cover and keep warm.

COOK'S TIP

One large fish looks spectacular, but it is
tricky to both cook and serve. If you prefer, buy four smaller fish and cook for a
shorter time, until just tender and cooked
through but not overdone.

2 Heat the remaining oil in the tin or
pan and fry the onions for 2–3
minutes until slightly softened. Add the
chilli and red and green peppers and
continue cooking for 3–4 minutes,
stirring occasionally, then add the garlic
and stir-fry for a further minute.

3 Blend the tomato purée with the
fish stock or water and stir into the
pan with the tomatoes, parsley, lemon
juice, paprika and seasoning. Simmer
gently without boiling for 15 minutes,
stirring occasionally.

4 Return the fish to the tin or pan
and cover with the sauce. Cook
for 10 minutes then add the olives and
cook for a further 5 minutes or until
just cooked through.

5 Transfer the fish to a serving dish
and pour the sauce over the top.
Allow to cool, then cover and chill
until completely cold. Serve cold with
bread and salad.

Baked or Grilled Spiced Whole Fish

INGREDIENTS

Serves 6

1kg/2¼lb bream, carp or pomfret, cleaned and scaled if necessary
1 fresh red chilli, seeded and ground, or 5ml/1 tsp chopped chilli from a jar
4 garlic cloves, crushed
2.5cm/1in fresh root ginger, peeled and sliced
4 spring onions, chopped
juice of ½ lemon
30ml/2 tbsp sunflower oil
salt

1 Rinse the fish and dry it well inside and out with absorbent kitchen paper. Slash two or three times through the fleshy part on each side of the fish.

2 Place the chilli, garlic, ginger and spring onions in a food processor and blend to a paste, or grind the mixture together with a pestle and mortar. Add the lemon juice and salt, then stir in the oil.

3 Spoon a little of the mixture inside the fish and pour the rest over the top. Turn the fish to coat it completely in the spice mixture and leave to marinate for at least an hour.

4 Preheat the grill. Place a long strip of double foil under the fish to support it and to make turning it over easier. Put on a rack in a grill pan and cook under the hot grill for 5 minutes on one side and 8 minutes on the second side, basting with the marinade during cooking. Serve with boiled rice.

Vinegar Chilli Fish

INGREDIENTS

Serves 2–3

2–3 mackerel, filleted
2–3 fresh red chillies, seeded
4 macadamia nuts or 8 almonds
1 red onion, quartered
2 garlic cloves, crushed
1cm/½in fresh root ginger, peeled and sliced
5ml/1 tsp ground turmeric
45ml/3 tbsp coconut or vegetable oil
45ml/3 tbsp wine vinegar
150ml/¼ pint/⅔ cup water
salt
deep-fried onions, to garnish
finely chopped fresh chilli, to garnish

1 Rinse the fish fillets in cold water and then dry them well on kitchen paper. Set aside.

2 Grind the chillies, nuts, onion, garlic, ginger, turmeric and 15ml/1 tbsp of the oil to a paste in a food processor or with a pestle and mortar. Heat the remaining oil in a frying pan and cook the paste for 1–2 minutes, without browning. Stir in the vinegar and water. Add salt to taste. Bring to the boil, then reduce to a simmer.

3 Place the fish fillets in the sauce. Cover and cook for 6–8 minutes, or until the fish is tender.

4 Lift the fish on to a plate and keep warm. Reduce the sauce by boiling rapidly for 1 minute. Pour over the fish and serve. Garnish with Deep-fried Onions and chopped chilli.

Mexican Spicy Fish

This is a typical Mexican dish.

INGREDIENTS

Serves 6

1.5kg/3–3½lb striped bass or any non-
   oily white fish, cut into 6 steaks
120ml/4fl oz/½cup corn oil
1 large onion, thinly sliced
2 garlic cloves, chopped
350g/12oz tomatoes, sliced
2 drained canned *jalapeño* chillies,
   rinsed and sliced

For the marinade

4 garlic cloves, crushed
5ml/1 tsp black peppercorns
5ml/1 tsp dried oregano
2.5ml/½tsp ground cumin
5ml/1 tsp ground *achiote* (annatto)
2.5ml/½tsp ground cinnamon
120ml/4fl oz/½cup mild white vinegar
salt
flat leaf parsley, to garnish

1 Arrange the fish steaks in a single layer in a shallow dish. Make the marinade. Using a pestle, grind the garlic and black peppercorns in a mortar. Add the dried oregano, cumin, *achiote* (annatto) and cinnamon and mix to a paste with the vinegar. Add salt to taste and spread the marinade on both sides of each of the fish steaks. Cover and leave in a cool place for 1 hour.

2 Select a flameproof dish large enough to hold the fish in a single layer and pour in enough of the oil to coat the bottom. Arrange the fish in the dish with any remaining marinade.

3 Top the fish with the onion, garlic, tomatoes and chillies and pour the rest of the oil over the top.

4 Cover the dish and cook over a low heat on top of the stove for 15–20 minutes, or until the fish is no longer translucent. Serve at once garnished with flat leaf parsley.

Citrus Fish with Chillies

INGREDIENTS

Serves 4
4 halibut or cod steaks or cutlets, about
  175g/6oz each
juice of 1 lemon
5ml/1 tsp garlic granules
5ml/1 tsp paprika
5ml/1 tsp ground cumin
4ml/¾ tsp dried tarragon
about 60ml/4 tbsp olive oil
flour, for dusting
300ml/½ pint/1¼ cups fish stock
2 red chillies, seeded and finely
  chopped
30ml/2 tbsp chopped fresh coriander
1 red onion, cut into rings
salt and freshly ground black pepper

1 Place the fish in a shallow bowl and mix together the lemon juice, garlic, paprika, cumin, tarragon and a little salt and pepper. Spoon over the lemon mixture, cover loosely with clear film and allow to marinate for a few hours or overnight in the fridge.

2 Gently heat all of the oil in a large non-stick frying pan, dust the fish with flour and then fry the fish for a few minutes each side, until golden brown all over.

3 Pour the fish stock around the fish, and simmer, covered for about 5 minutes until the fish is thoroughly cooked through.

4 Add the chopped red chillies and 15ml/1 tbsp of the coriander to the pan. Simmer for 5 minutes.

5 Transfer the fish and sauce to a serving plate and keep warm.

6 Wipe the pan, heat some olive oil and stir fry the onion rings until speckled brown. Scatter over the fish with the remaining chopped coriander and serve at once.

King Prawns in Curry Sauce

INGREDIENTS

Serves 4

450g/1lb raw king prawns
600ml/1 pint/2½ cups water
3 thin slices fresh root ginger
10ml/2 tsp curry powder
2 garlic cloves, crushed
15g/½ oz/1 tbsp butter or margarine
60ml/4 tbsp ground almonds
1 green chilli, seeded and finely
  chopped
45ml/3 tbsp single cream
salt and freshly ground black pepper

For the vegetables

15ml/1 tbsp mustard oil
15ml/1 tbsp vegetable oil
1 onion, sliced
½ red pepper, seeded and thinly sliced
½ green pepper, seeded and thinly
  sliced
1 christophene, peeled, stoned and cut
  into strips
salt and freshly ground black pepper

1 Shell the prawns and place shells in a saucepan with the water and ginger. Simmer, uncovered, for 15 minutes until reduced by half. Strain into a jug and discard the shells.

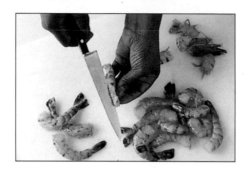

2 Devein the prawns, place in a bowl and season with the curry powder, garlic and salt and pepper and set aside.

3 Heat the mustard and vegetable oils in a large frying pan, add all the vegetables and stir fry for 5 minutes. Season with salt and pepper, spoon into a serving dish and keep warm.

4 Wipe out the frying pan, then melt the butter or margarine and sauté the prawns for about 5 minutes until pink. Spoon over the bed of vegetables, cover and keep warm.

5 Add the ground almonds and chilli to the pan, stir fry for a few seconds and then add the reserved stock and bring to the boil. Reduce the heat, stir in the cream and simmer for a few minutes, without boiling.

6 Pour the sauce over the vegetables and prawns before serving.

Fried Fish in Green Chilli Sauce

INGREDIENTS

Serves 4

4 medium pomfret
juice of 1 lemon
5ml/1 tsp garlic granules
salt and freshly ground black pepper
vegetable oil, for shallow frying

For the coconut sauce

450ml/¾ pint/1⅞ cups water
2 thin slices fresh root ginger
25–40g/1–1½ oz creamed coconut
30ml/2 tbsp vegetable oil
1 red onion, sliced
2 garlic cloves, crushed
1 green chilli, seeded and thinly sliced
15ml/1 tbsp chopped fresh coriander
salt and freshly ground black pepper

1 Cut the fish in half and sprinkle inside and out with the lemon juice. Season with the garlic granules and salt and pepper and set aside to marinate for a few hours.

2 Heat a little oil in a large frying pan. Pat away the excess lemon juice from the fish, fry in the oil for 10 minutes, turning once. Set aside.

3 To make the sauce, place the water in a saucepan with the slices of ginger, bring to the boil and simmer until the liquid is reduced to just over 300ml/½ pint/1¼ cups. Take out the ginger and reserve, then add the creamed coconut to the pan and stir until the coconut has melted.

4 Heat the oil in a wok or large pan and fry the onion and garlic for 2–3 minutes. Add the reserved ginger and coconut stock, the chilli and coriander, stir well and then gently add the fish. Simmer for 10 minutes, until the fish is cooked through. Transfer the fish to a warmed serving plate, adjust the seasoning for the sauce and pour over the fish. Serve immediately.

Chilli Crabs

There are variations on this recipe all over Asia, but all are hot and spicy. This delicious dish owes its spiciness and flavour to chillies, ginger and shrimp paste.

INGREDIENTS

Serves 4

2 cooked crabs, about 675g/1½lb
1cm/½in cube shrimp paste
2 garlic cloves
2 fresh red chillies, seeded, or 5ml/
  1 tsp chopped chilli from a jar
1cm/½in fresh root ginger, peeled
  and sliced
60ml/4 tbsp sunflower oil
300ml/½ pint/1¼ cups tomato ketchup
15ml/1 tbsp dark brown sugar
150ml/¼ pint/⅔ cup warm water
4 spring onions, chopped, to garnish
cucumber chunks and hot toast,
  to serve (optional)

1 Remove the large claws of one crab and turn on to its back, with the head facing away from you. Use your thumbs to push the body up from the main shell. Discard the stomach sac and "dead men's fingers", i.e. lungs and any green matter. Leave the creamy brown meat in the shell and cut the shell in half, with a cleaver or strong knife. Cut the body section in half and crack the claws with a sharp blow from a hammer or cleaver. Avoid splintering the claws. Repeat with the other crab.

2 Grind the shrimp paste, garlic, chillies and ginger to a paste with a pestle and mortar.

3 Heat a wok and add the oil. Fry the spice paste, stirring it all the time, without browning.

4 Stir in the tomato ketchup, sugar and water and mix the sauce well. When just boiling, add all the crab pieces and toss in the sauce until well-coated and hot. Serve in a large bowl, sprinkled with the spring onions. Place in the centre of the table for everyone to help themselves. Accompany this finger-licking dish with cool cucumber chunks and hot toast for mopping up the sauce, if you like.

Spicy Prawns with Cornmeal

These crispy fried prawns with a cornmeal coating and a cheesy topping are truly delicious when served with a spicy tomato salsa and lime wedges to ease the heat.

INGREDIENTS

Serves 4

115g/4oz/³/₄ cup cornmeal
5–10ml/1–2 tsp cayenne pepper
2.5ml/½ tsp ground cumin
5ml/1 tsp salt
30ml/2 tbsp chopped fresh coriander
　or parsley
900g/2lb large raw prawns, peeled and
　deveined
flour, for dredging
¼ cup vegetable oil
115g/4oz/1 cup grated
　Cheddar cheese

To serve
lime wedges
tomato salsa

1 Preheat the grill. In a mixing bowl, combine the cornmeal, cayenne, cumin, salt and coriander or parsley.

2 Coat the prawns lightly in flour, then dip them in water and roll them in the cornmeal mixture to coat.

3 Heat the oil in a non-stick frying pan. When hot, add the prawns, in batches if necessary. Cook them until they are opaque throughout, for about 2–3 minutes on each side. Drain on kitchen paper.

4 Place the prawns in a large baking dish, or in individual dishes. Sprinkle the cheese evenly over the top. Grill about 8cm/3in from the heat until the cheese melts, for about 2–3 minutes. Serve immediately, with lime wedges and tomato salsa.

Prawns in Spiced Coconut Sauce

Spices, chillies and herbs make a
fragrant sauce for this dish.

INGREDIENTS

Serves 4
24–30 large raw prawns
spice seasoning, for dusting
juice of 1 lemon
30ml/2 tbsp butter or margarine
1 onion, chopped
2 garlic cloves, crushed
30ml/2 tbsp tomato purée
2.5ml/½ tsp dried thyme
2.5ml/½ tsp ground cinnamon
15ml/1 tbsp chopped fresh coriander
½ hot chilli pepper, chopped
175g/6oz frozen or canned sweetcorn
300ml/½ pint/1¼ cups coconut milk
chopped fresh coriander, to garnish

1 Sprinkle the prawns with spice
seasoning and lemon juice and
marinate in a cool place for an hour.

2 Melt the butter or margarine in a
saucepan, fry the onion and garlic
for 5 minutes, until slightly softened.
Add the prawns and cook for a few
minutes, stirring occasionally until
cooked through and pink.

3 Transfer the prawns, onion and
garlic to a bowl, leaving behind
some of the buttery liquid. Add the
tomato purée to the pan and cook
over a low heat, stirring thoroughly.
Add the thyme, cinnamon, coriander
and hot pepper and stir well.

4 Blend the sweetcorn (reserving
15ml/1 tbsp) in a blender or food
processor with the coconut milk. Add
to the pan and simmer until reduced.
Add the prawns and reserved corn, and
simmer for 5 minutes. Serve hot,
garnished with coriander.

> ——— COOK'S TIP ———
>
> If you use raw king prawns, make a stock
> from the shells and use in place of some of
> the coconut milk.

Curried Prawns and Saltfish

Shrimp paste and spices add tasty
flavour to this fish dish.

INGREDIENTS

Serves 4
450g/1lb raw prawns, peeled
15ml/1 tbsp spice seasoning
25g/1oz/2 tbsp butter or margarine
15ml/1 tbsp olive oil
2 shallots, finely chopped
1 garlic clove, crushed
350g/12oz okra, topped, tailed and cut
  into 2.5cm/1in lengths
5ml/1 tsp curry powder
10ml/2 tsp shrimp paste
15ml/1 tbsp chopped fresh coriander
15ml/1 tbsp lemon juice
175g/6oz prepared saltfish (see Cook's
  Tip), shredded

1 Season the prawns with the spice
seasoning and leave to marinate in a
cool place for about 1 hour.

2 Heat the butter or margarine and
olive oil in a large frying pan or
wok over a moderate heat and stir-fry
the shallots and garlic for 5 minutes.
Add the okra, curry powder and shrimp
paste, stir well and cook for about
10 minutes, until the okra is tender.

3 Add 30ml/2 tbsp water, coriander,
lemon juice, prawns and saltfish,
and cook gently for 5–10 minutes.
Adjust the seasoning and serve hot.

> ——— COOK'S TIP ———
>
> Soak the saltfish for 12 hours, changing the
> water two or three times. Rinse, bring to
> the boil in fresh water, then cool.

Pineapple Curry with Prawns and Mussels

The delicate sweet and sour flavour of this curry comes from the pineapple and although it seems an odd combination, it is rather delicious. Use the freshest shellfish that you can find.

INGREDIENTS

Serves 4–6
600ml/1 pint/2½ cups coconut milk
30ml/2 tbsp red curry paste
30ml/2 tbsp fish sauce
15ml/1 tbsp granulated sugar
225g/8oz king prawns, shelled
    and deveined
450g/1lb mussels, cleaned and
    beards removed
175g/6oz fresh pineapple, finely
    crushed or chopped
5 kaffir lime leaves, torn
2 red chillies, chopped, to garnish
coriander leaves, to garnish

1 In a large saucepan, bring half the coconut milk to the boil and heat, stirring, until it separates.

2 Add the red curry paste and cook until fragrant. Add the fish sauce and sugar and continue to cook for a few moments.

3 Stir in the rest of the coconut milk and bring back to the boil. Add the king prawns, mussels, pineapple and kaffir lime leaves.

4 Reheat until boiling and then simmer for 3–5 minutes, until the prawns are cooked and the mussels have opened. Remove any mussels that have not opened and discard. Serve garnished with chopped red chillies and coriander leaves.

Curried Prawns in Coconut Milk

A curry-like dish where the prawns are cooked in a spicy coconut gravy.

INGREDIENTS

Serves 4–6
600ml/1 pint/2½ cups coconut milk
30ml/2 tbsp yellow curry paste (see
    Cook's Tip)
15ml/1 tbsp fish sauce
2.5ml/½ tsp salt
5ml/1 tsp granulated sugar
450g/1lb king prawns, shelled, tails left
    intact and deveined
225g/8oz cherry tomatoes
juice of ½ lime, to serve
2 red chillies, cut into strips, to garnish
coriander leaves, to garnish

1 Put half the coconut milk into a pan or wok and bring to the boil.

2 Add the yellow curry paste to the coconut milk, stir until it disperses, then simmer for about 10 minutes.

3 Add the fish sauce, salt, sugar and remaining coconut milk. Simmer for another 5 minutes.

4 Add the prawns and cherry tomatoes. Simmer very gently for about 5 minutes until the prawns are pink and tender.

5 Serve sprinkled with lime juice and garnish with chillies and coriander.

--- COOK'S TIP ---

To make yellow curry paste, process together 6–8 yellow chillies, 1 chopped lemon grass stalk, 4 peeled shallots, 4 garlic cloves, 15ml/1 tbsp peeled chopped fresh root ginger, 5ml/1 tsp coriander seeds, 5ml/1 tsp mustard powder, 5ml/1 tsp salt, 2.5ml/½ tsp ground cinnamon, 15ml/1 tbsp light brown sugar and 30ml/2 tbsp oil in a blender or food processor. When a paste has formed, transfer to a glass jar and keep in the fridge.

MEAT & POULTRY

Tex-Mex Baked Potatoes with Chilli

INGREDIENTS

Serves 4

2 large potatoes
15ml/1 tbsp oil
1 garlic clove, crushed
1 small onion, chopped
½ red pepper, seeded and chopped
225g/8oz lean minced beef
½ fresh red chilli, seeded and chopped
5ml/1 tsp ground cumin
pinch of cayenne pepper
200g/7oz can chopped tomatoes
30ml/2 tbsp tomato purée
2.5ml/½ tsp dried oregano
2.5ml/½ tsp dried marjoram
200g/7oz can red kidney beans
15ml/1 tbsp chopped fresh coriander
60ml/4 tbsp soured cream
salt and ground black pepper
chopped fresh parsley, to garnish

1 Preheat the oven to 220°C/425°F/ Gas 7. Oil the potatoes and pierce with skewers. Bake for 30 minutes.

2 Heat the oil in a pan and add the garlic, onion and pepper. Fry gently for 4–5 minutes until softened.

3 Add the minced beef and fry until it is browned all over, then stir in the chopped chilli, ground cumin, cayenne pepper, tomatoes, tomato purée, 60ml/4 tbsp water and the herbs. Cover and simmer for about 25 minutes, stirring occasionally.

--- VARIATION ---

For a lower fat topping, use natural yogurt instead of soured cream.

4 Drain the kidney beans and add to the pan. Cook for 5 minutes, turn off the heat and stir in the chopped coriander. Season well and set aside.

5 Cut the baked potatoes in half and place one half in each of four serving bowls. Top them with the chilli beef mixture and a dollop of soured cream and garnish with plenty of chopped fresh parsley.

Spicy Meatballs

Serve these Indonesian meatballs
with a sambal or a spicy sauce.

INGREDIENTS

Makes 24
1 large onion, roughly chopped
1–2 fresh red chillies, seeded
  and chopped
2 garlic cloves, crushed
1cm/½in cube shrimp paste
15ml/1 tbsp coriander seeds
5ml/1 tsp cumin seeds
450g/1lb lean minced beef
10ml/2 tsp dark soy sauce
5ml/1 tsp dark brown sugar
juice of ½ lemon
a little beaten egg
oil for shallow-frying
salt and freshly ground black pepper
fresh coriander sprigs, to garnish

1 Put the onions, chillies, garlic and
shrimp paste in a food processor.
Process but do not over-chop or the
onion will become too wet and spoil
the consistency of the meatballs. Dry-
fry the coriander and cumin seeds in a
preheated pan for about 1 minute, to
release the aroma. Do not brown.
Grind with a pestle and mortar.

2 Put the meat in a large bowl. Stir
in the onion mixture. Add the
ground coriander and cumin, soy
sauce, seasoning, sugar and lemon
juice. Bind with a little beaten egg and
shape into small, even-size balls.

3 Chill the meatballs briefly to firm
up, if necessary. Fry in shallow oil,
turning often, until cooked through
and browned. This will take
4–5 minutes, depending on their size.

4 Remove from the pan, drain well
on kitchen paper and serve,
garnished with coriander sprigs.

Beef and Aubergine Curry

INGREDIENTS

Serves 6

120ml/4fl oz/½ cup sunflower oil
2 onions, thinly sliced
2.5cm/1in fresh root ginger, sliced and
    cut in matchsticks
1 garlic clove, crushed
2 fresh red chillies, seeded and very
    finely sliced
2.5cm/1in fresh turmeric, peeled and
    crushed, or 5ml/1 tsp
    ground turmeric
1 lemon grass stem, lower part sliced
    finely, top bruised
675g/1½ lb braising steak, cut in even-
    size strips
400ml/14fl oz can coconut milk
300ml/½ pint/1¼ cups water
1 aubergine, sliced and patted dry
5ml/1 tsp tamarind pulp, soaked in
    60ml/4 tbsp warm water
salt and freshly ground black pepper
finely sliced chilli and deep-fried
    onions, to garnish
boiled rice, to serve

1 Heat half the oil and fry the
onions, ginger and garlic until they
give off a rich aroma. Add the chillies,
turmeric and the lower part of the
lemon grass. Push to one side and then
turn up the heat and add the steak,
stirring until the meat changes colour.

—————— COOK'S TIP ——————

If you want to make this curry, *Gulai
Terung Dengan Daging,* ahead, prepare to
the end of step 2 and finish later.

2 Add the coconut milk, water,
lemon grass top and seasoning to
taste. Cover and simmer gently for
1½ hours, or until the meat is tender.

3 Towards the end of the cooking
time heat the remaining oil in a
frying pan. Fry the aubergine slices
until brown on both sides.

4 Add the browned aubergine slices
to the beef curry and cook for a
further 15 minutes. Stir gently from
time to time. Strain the tamarind and
stir the juice into the curry. Taste and
adjust the seasoning. Put into a warm
serving dish. Garnish with the sliced
chilli and deep-fried onions and serve
with boiled rice.

Beef Enchiladas

Ingredients

Serves 4

900g/2lb chuck steak
15ml/1 tbsp vegetable oil, plus extra
  for frying
5ml/1 tsp salt
5ml/1 tsp dried oregano
2.5ml/½ tsp ground cumin
1 onion, quartered
2 garlic cloves, crushed
1 litre/1¾ pints/4 cups enchilada sauce
12 corn tortillas
115g/4oz/1 cup grated cheese
chopped spring onions, to garnish
soured cream, to serve

2 Place in a baking dish and bake for 3 hours, until the meat is tender enough to shred. Remove from the foil and shred the meat using two forks.

3 Stir 120ml/4fl oz/½ cup of the enchilada sauce into the beef. Spoon a thin layer of enchilada sauce on the bottom of a rectangular baking dish, or in four individual dishes.

5 Put a 1cm/½in layer of vegetable oil in a second frying pan and heat until hot but not smoking. With tongs, lower a tortilla into the oil; the temperature is correct if it just sizzles. Cook for 2 seconds, then turn and cook the other side for 2 seconds. Lift out, drain over the pan, and then transfer to the pan with the sauce. Dip in the sauce just to coat both sides.

6 Transfer the softened tortilla immediately to a plate. Spread about 2–3 spoonfuls of the beef mixture down the centre of the tortilla. Roll it up and place the filled tortilla seam-side down in the prepared dish. Repeat this process for all the remaining tortillas.

7 Spoon the remaining sauce from the frying pan over the beef enchiladas, spreading it right down to the ends. Sprinkle the grated cheese down the centre.

8 Bake the enchiladas until the cheese topping just melts, for about 10–15 minutes. Sprinkle with chopped spring onions and serve at once, with soured cream on the side.

1 Preheat the oven to 160°C/325°F/ Gas 3. Place the meat on a sheet of foil and rub it all over with the oil. Sprinkle both sides with the salt, oregano and cumin and rub in well. Add the onion and garlic. Top with another sheet of foil and roll up to seal the edges, leaving room for some steam expansion during cooking.

4 Place the remaining sauce in a frying pan and warm gently.

COOK'S TIP

For a quicker recipe, use minced beef. Fry in a little oil with chopped onion and garlic, until browned all over. Continue the recipe from step 3.

Spicy Meat Fritters

INGREDIENTS

Makes 30

450g/1lb potatoes, boiled and drained
450g/1lb lean minced beef
1 onion, quartered
1 bunch spring onions, chopped
3 garlic cloves, crushed
5ml/1 tsp ground nutmeg
15ml/1 tbsp coriander seeds, dry-fried
   and ground
10ml/2 tsp cumin seeds, dry-fried
   and ground
4 eggs, beaten
oil for shallow-frying
salt and freshly ground black pepper

1 While the potatoes are still warm, mash them in the pan until they are well broken up. Add to the minced beef and mix well together.

2 Finely chop the onion, spring onions and garlic. Add to the meat with the ground nutmeg, coriander and cumin. Stir in enough beaten egg to give a soft consistency which can be formed into fritters. Season to taste.

3 Heat the oil in a large frying pan. Using a dessertspoon, scoop out 6–8 oval-shaped fritters and drop them into the hot oil. Allow to set, so that they keep their shape (this will take about 3 minutes) and then turn over and cook for a further minute.

4 Drain well on kitchen paper and keep warm while cooking the remaining fritters.

Barbecued Pork Spareribs

INGREDIENTS

Serves 4

1kg/2¼ lb pork spareribs
1 onion
2 garlic cloves
2.5cm/1in fresh root ginger
75ml/3fl oz/⅓ cup dark soy sauce
1–2 fresh red chillies, seeded
   and chopped
5ml/1 tsp tamarind pulp, soaked in
   75ml/3fl oz/⅓ cup water
15–30ml/1–2 tbsp dark brown sugar
30ml/2 tbsp groundnut oil
salt and freshly ground black pepper

1 Wipe the pork ribs and place them in a wok, wide frying pan or large flameproof casserole.

2 Finely chop the onion, crush the garlic and peel and slice the ginger. Blend the soy sauce, onion, garlic, ginger and chopped chillies together to a paste in a food processor or with a pestle and mortar. Strain the tamarind and reserve the juice. Add the tamarind juice, brown sugar, oil and seasoning to taste to the onion mixture and mix well together.

3 Pour the sauce over the ribs and toss well to coat. Bring to the boil and then simmer, uncovered and stirring frequently, for 30 minutes. Add extra water if necessary.

4 Put the ribs on a rack in a roasting tin, place under a preheated grill, on a barbecue or in the oven at 200°C/400°F/Gas 6 and continue cooking until the ribs are tender, about 20 minutes, depending on the thickness of the ribs. Baste the ribs with the sauce and turn them over from time to time.

Sweet and Sour Pork

INGREDIENTS

Serves 4

350g/12oz lean pork
1.5ml/¼ tsp salt and 2.5ml/½ tsp
   ground Szechuan peppercorns
15ml/1 tbsp Chinese rice wine
115g/4oz bamboo shoots
30ml/2 tbsp plain flour
1 egg, lightly beaten
vegetable oil, for frying
15ml/1 tbsp vegetable oil
1 garlic clove, finely chopped
1 spring onion, cut into short sections
1 small green pepper, diced finely
1 fresh red chilli, seeded
   and shredded
15ml/1 tbsp light soy sauce
30ml/2 tbsp light brown sugar
45ml/3 tbsp rice vinegar
15ml/1 tbsp tomato purée
about 120ml/4fl oz/½ cup stock

1 Using a sharp knife, cut the lean pork into small bite-size cubes. Marinate with the salt, ground peppercorns and Chinese wine for about 15–20 minutes.

2 Cut the bamboo shoots into small cubes about the same size as the pork pieces.

3 Dust the pork with flour, dip in the beaten egg, and coat with more flour. Deep-fry in moderately hot oil for 3–4 minutes, stirring to separate the pieces. Remove.

4 Reheat the oil, add the pork and bamboo shoots and fry for 1 minute, or until golden. Drain.

5 Heat 15ml/1 tbsp oil and add the garlic, spring onion, pepper and chilli. Stir-fry for 30–40 seconds, then add the seasonings with the stock. Bring to the boil, then add the pork and bamboo shoots.

Caribbean Lamb Curry

This popular national dish of Jamaica is known as Curry Goat, although goat meat or lamb can be used to make it.

INGREDIENTS

Serves 4–6
900g/2lb boned leg of lamb
60ml/4 tbsp curry powder
3 garlic cloves, crushed
1 large onion, chopped
4 thyme sprigs or 5ml/1 tsp
  dried thyme
3 bay leaves
5ml/1 tsp ground allspice
30ml/2 tbsp vegetable oil
50g/2oz/4 tbsp butter or margarine
900ml/1½ pints/3¾ cups stock or water
1 fresh hot chilli pepper, chopped
cooked rice, to serve
coriander sprigs, to garnish

1 Cut the meat into 5cm/2in cubes, discarding any excess fat and gristle.

2 Place the lamb, curry powder, garlic, onion, thyme, bay leaves, allspice and oil in a large bowl and mix. Marinate in the fridge for at least 3 hours or overnight.

3 Melt the butter or margarine in a large heavy saucepan, add the seasoned lamb and fry over a moderate heat for about 10 minutes, turning the meat frequently.

4 Stir in the stock and chilli and bring to the boil. Reduce the heat, cover the pan and simmer for 1½ hours, or until the meat is tender. Serve, garnished with coriander, with rice.

COOK'S TIP

Try goat, or mutton, if you can and enjoy a robust curry.

Khara Masala Lamb

Whole spices are used in this curry so you should warn the diners of their presence in advance! It is delicious when served with freshly baked naan bread or a rice accompaniment. This dish is best made with good-quality spring lamb.

INGREDIENTS

Serves 4
75ml/5 tbsp corn oil
2 onions, chopped
5ml/1 tsp shredded ginger
5ml/1 tsp sliced garlic
6 whole dried red chillies
3 cardamom pods
2 cinnamon sticks
6 black peppercorns
3 cloves
2.5ml/½ tsp salt
450g/1lb boned leg of lamb, cubed
600ml/1 pint/2½ cups water
2 fresh green chillies, sliced
30ml/2 tbsp chopped fresh coriander

1 Heat the oil in a large saucepan. Lower the heat slightly and fry the onions until they are lightly browned.

2 Add half the ginger and half the garlic and stir well.

3 Throw in half the red chillies, the cardamoms, cinnamon, peppercorns, cloves and salt.

4 Add the lamb and fry over a medium heat. Stir continuously with a semi-circular movement, using a wooden spoon to scrape the bottom of the pan. Continue in this way for about 5 minutes.

5 Pour in the water, cover with a lid and cook over a medium-low heat for 35–40 minutes, or until the water has evaporated and the meat is tender.

6 Add the rest of the shredded ginger, sliced garlic and the whole dried red chillies, along with the sliced fresh green chillies and the fresh chopped coriander.

COOK'S TIP

The action of stirring the meat and spices together using a semi-circular motion, as described in step 4, is called bhoono-ing. It ensures that the meat becomes well-coated and combined with the spice mixture before the cooking liquid is added.

---

7 Continue to stir over the heat until you see some free oil on the sides of the pan. Transfer to a serving dish and serve immediately.

Spatchcocked Devilled Poussins

English mustard adds a hot touch to the spice paste used in this tasty recipe.

INGREDIENTS

Serves 4

15ml/1 tbsp English mustard powder
15ml/1 tbsp paprika
15ml/1 tbsp ground cumin
20ml/4 tsp tomato ketchup
15ml/1 tbsp lemon juice
65g/2½oz/5 tbsp butter, melted
4 poussins, about 450g/1lb each
salt

1 In a mixing bowl, combine the English mustard, paprika, ground cumin, tomato ketchup, lemon juice and salt. Mix together until smooth, then gradually stir in the melted butter until incorporated.

2 Using game shears or a strong pair of kitchen scissors, split each poussin along one side of the backbone, then cut down the other side of the backbone to remove it.

3 Open out a poussin, skin-side uppermost, then press down firmly with the heel of your hand. Pass a long skewer through one leg and out through the other to secure the bird open and flat. Repeat with the remaining birds.

4 Spread the spicy mustard mixture evenly over the skin of each of the poussins. Cover them loosely and leave in a cool place for at least 2 hours. Preheat the grill.

5 Place the prepared poussins, skin-side uppermost, on a grill rack and grill them for about 12 minutes. Turn the birds over and baste with any juices in the pan. Cook the poussins for a further 7 minutes, until all the juices run clear.

COOK'S TIP

Spatchcocked poussins cook very well on the barbecue. Make sure that the coals are very hot, then cook the birds for about 15–20 minutes, turning and basting them frequently as they cook.

Bon-bon Chicken with Spicy Sesame

In this recipe, the chicken meat is tenderized by being beaten with a stick (called a "bon" in Chinese) – hence the name for this very popular Szechuan dish.

INGREDIENTS

Serves 6–8

1 whole chicken, about 1kg/2¼lb
1.2 litres/2 pints/5 cups water
15ml/1 tbsp sesame oil
shredded cucumber, to garnish

For the sauce

30ml/2 tbsp light soy sauce
5ml/1 tsp sugar
15ml/1 tbsp finely chopped
   spring onions
5ml/1 tsp red chilli oil
2.5ml/½ tsp Szechuan peppercorns
5ml/1 tsp white sesame seeds
30ml/2 tbsp sesame paste, or
   30ml/2 tbsp peanut butter creamed
   with a little sesame oil

1 Clean the chicken well. In a wok or saucepan bring the water to a rolling boil, add the chicken, reduce the heat and cook under cover for 40–45 minutes. Remove the chicken and immerse in cold water to cool.

2 After at least 1 hour, remove the chicken and drain; dry well with kitchen paper and brush with sesame oil. Carve the meat from the legs, wings and breast and pull the meat off the rest of the bones.

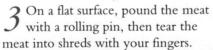

3 On a flat surface, pound the meat with a rolling pin, then tear the meat into shreds with your fingers.

4 Place the meat in a dish with the shredded cucumber around the edge. In a bowl, mix together all the sauce ingredients, keeping a few spring onions to garnish. Pour over the chicken and serve.

COOK'S TIP ➙

To make chilli oil, slit and blanch chillies, pack into sterilized jars and fill with oil. Leave for 2 weeks.

Spicy Fried Chicken

This crispy chicken is superb hot or cold. Served with a salad or vegetables, it makes a delicious lunch and is ideal for picnics or snacks too.

INGREDIENTS

Serves 4–6
4 chicken drumsticks
4 chicken thighs
10ml/2 tsp curry powder
2.5ml/½ tsp garlic granules
2.5ml/½ tsp ground black pepper
2.5ml/½ tsp paprika
about 300ml/½ pint/1¼ cups milk
oil, for deep frying
50g/2oz/4 tbsp plain flour
salt
salad leaves, to serve

1 Place the chicken pieces in a large bowl and sprinkle with the curry powder, garlic granules, black pepper, paprika and salt. Rub the spices well into the chicken, then cover and leave to marinate in a cool place for at least 2 hours, or overnight in the fridge.

2 Preheat the oven to 180°C/350°F/ Gas 4. Pour enough milk into the bowl to cover the chicken and leave to stand for a further 15 minutes.

3 Heat the oil in a large saucepan or deep-fat fryer and tip the flour on to a plate. Shake off excess milk, dip each piece of chicken in flour and fry two or three pieces at a time until golden, but not cooked. Continue until all the chicken pieces are fried.

4 Remove with a slotted spoon, place the chicken pieces on a baking tray, and bake for about 30 minutes. Serve hot or cold with salad.

Spicy Chicken with Coconut

Traditionally, the chicken pieces for this Indonesian dish would be part-cooked by frying, but roasting in the oven is just as successful. This recipe is unusual in that it does not contain any chillies or turmeric, but galangal, lemon grass, coriander and lime leaves add a deliciously spicy flavour.

INGREDIENTS

1.5kg/3–3½lb chicken or 4 chicken quarters
4 garlic cloves
1 onion, sliced
4 macadamia nuts or 8 almonds
15ml/1 tbsp coriander seeds, dry-fried, or 5ml/1 tsp ground coriander
45ml/3 tbsp oil
2.5cm/1in fresh galangal, peeled and bruised
2 lemon grass stems, fleshy part bruised
3 lime leaves
2 bay leaves
5ml/1 tsp sugar
600ml/1 pint/2½ cups coconut milk
salt
boiled rice and deep-fried onions, to serve

1 Preheat the oven to 190°C/375°F/ Gas 5. Cut the chicken into four or eight pieces. Season with salt. Put in an oiled roasting tin and cook in the oven for 25–30 minutes. Meanwhile prepare the sauce.

2 Grind the garlic, onion, nuts and coriander to a fine paste in a food processor or with a pestle and mortar. Heat the oil and fry the paste to bring out the flavour. Do not allow it to brown.

3 Add the part-cooked chicken pieces to a wok together with the galangal, lemon grass, lime and bay leaves, sugar, coconut milk and salt to taste. Mix well to coat in the sauce.

4 Bring to the boil and then reduce the heat and simmer gently for 30–40 minutes, uncovered, until the chicken is tender and the coconut sauce is reduced and thickened. Stir the mixture occasionally during cooking.

5 Just before serving, remove the bruised galangal and lemon grass. Serve with boiled rice sprinkled with crisp deep-fried onions.

Barbecued Jerk Chicken

Jerk refers to the blend of herb and spice seasoning rubbed into meat, before it is roasted over charcoal sprinkled with pimiento berries. In Jamaica, jerk seasoning was originally used only for pork, but jerked chicken is equally good.

INGREDIENTS

Serves 4
8 chicken pieces

For the marinade
5ml/1 tsp ground allspice
5ml/1 tsp ground cinnamon
5ml/1 tsp dried thyme
1.5ml/¼ tsp freshly grated nutmeg
10ml/2 tsp demerara sugar
2 garlic cloves, crushed
15ml/1 tbsp finely chopped onion
15ml/1 tbsp chopped spring onion
15ml/1 tbsp vinegar
30ml/2 tbsp oil
15ml/1 tbsp lime juice
1 hot chilli pepper, chopped
salt and freshly ground black pepper
salad leaves, to serve

1 Combine all the marinade ingredients in a small bowl. Using a fork, mash them together well to form a thick paste.

2 Lay the chicken pieces on a plate or board and make several lengthways slits in the flesh. Rub the seasoning all over the chicken and into the slits.

3 Place the chicken pieces in a dish, cover with clear film and marinate overnight in the fridge.

4 Shake off any excess seasoning from the chicken. Brush with oil and either place on a baking sheet or on a barbecue grill if barbecuing. Cook under a preheated grill for 45 minutes, turning often. Or, if barbecuing, light the coals and when ready, cook over the coals for 30 minutes, turning often. Serve hot with salad leaves.

COOK'S TIP

The flavour is best if you marinate the chicken overnight. Sprinkle the charcoal with aromatic herbs such as bay leaves for even more flavour.

Blackened Hot Chicken Breasts

INGREDIENTS

Serves 6
6 skinless boneless chicken breasts
75g/3oz/6 tbsp butter or margarine
5ml/1 tsp garlic powder
10ml/2 tsp onion powder
5ml/1 tsp cayenne pepper
10ml/2 tsp sweet paprika
7.5ml/1½ tsp salt
2.5ml/½ tsp white pepper
5ml/1 tsp ground black pepper
1.5ml/¼ tsp ground cumin
5ml/1 tsp dried thyme

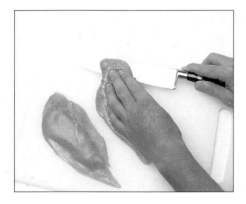

1 Slice each chicken breast piece in half horizontally, making two pieces of about the same thickness. Flatten slightly with the heel of your hand.

2 Melt the butter or margarine in a small saucepan.

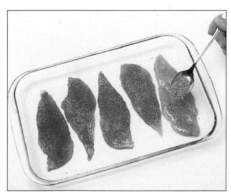

3 Combine all the remaining ingredients in a shallow bowl and stir to blend well. Brush the chicken pieces on both sides with melted butter or margarine, then sprinkle evenly with the seasoning mixture.

4 Heat a large heavy frying pan over a high heat until a drop of water sprinkled on the surface sizzles. This will take 5–8 minutes.

5 Drizzle 5ml/1 tsp melted butter on each chicken piece. Place them in the pan in an even layer, two or three at a time. Cook for 2–3 minutes until the underside begins to blacken. Turn and cook the other side for another 2–3 minutes. Serve hot.

Chicken Sauce Piquante

Red chilli peppers add heat to this Cajun recipe. Sauce Piquante is commonly used in lots of recipes to liven up meat and fish and give meals a spicy taste.

INGREDIENTS

Serves 4
4 chicken legs or 2 legs and 2 breasts
75ml/5 tbsp oil
50g/2oz/½ cup plain flour
1 onion, chopped
2 celery sticks, sliced
1 green pepper, seeded and diced
2 garlic cloves, crushed
1 bay leaf
2.5ml/½ tsp dried thyme
2.5ml/½ tsp dried oregano
1–2 red chilli peppers, seeded and
  finely chopped
400g/14oz can tomatoes, chopped,
  with their juice
300ml/½ pint/1¼ cups chicken stock
salt and ground black pepper
watercress, to garnish
boiled potatoes, to serve

COOK'S TIP

If you prefer to err on the side of caution with chilli heat, use just 1 chilli pepper and hot up the seasoning at the end with a dash or two of Tabasco sauce.

1 Halve the chicken legs through the joint, or the breasts across the middle, to give eight pieces.

2 In a heavy frying pan, fry the chicken pieces in the oil until brown on all sides, lifting them out and setting them aside as they are done.

3 Strain the oil from the pan into a heavy flameproof casserole. Heat it and stir in the flour. Stir constantly over a low heat until the roux is the colour of peanut butter.

4 As soon as the roux reaches the right stage, tip in the onion, celery and pepper and stir over the heat for 2–3 minutes.

5 Add the garlic, bay leaf, thyme, oregano and chilli pepper(s). Stir for 1 minute, then turn down the heat and stir in the tomatoes with their juice.

6 Return the casserole to the heat and gradually stir in the stock. Add the chicken pieces, cover and leave to simmer for 45 minutes, until the chicken is tender.

7 If there is too much sauce or it is too runny, remove the lid for the last 10–15 minutes of the cooking time and raise the heat a little.

8 Check the seasoning and serve garnished with watercress and accompanied by boiled potatoes, or perhaps rice or pasta, and a green vegetable or salad of your choice.

VARIATION

Any kind of meat, poultry or fish can be served with Sauce Piquante. Just cook the meat or fish first, then serve it with plenty of the sauce.

Tandoori Chicken

INGREDIENTS

Serves 4

4 chicken quarters
175ml/6fl oz/³/₄ cup natural
 low-fat yogurt
5ml/1 tsp garam masala
5ml/1 tsp ginger pulp
5ml/1 tsp garlic pulp
7.5ml/1½ tsp chilli powder
1.5ml/¼ tsp turmeric
5ml/1 tsp ground coriander
15ml/1 tbsp lemon juice
5ml/1 tsp salt
few drops red food colouring
30ml/2 tbsp corn oil
mixed salad leaves, lime wedges and
 1 tomato, quartered, to garnish

1 Skin, rinse and pat dry the chicken quarters. Make two slits into the flesh of each piece, place them in a dish and set aside.

2 Mix together the yogurt, garam masala, ginger, garlic, chilli powder, turmeric, ground coriander, lemon juice, salt, red colouring and oil, and beat so that all the ingredients are well mixed together.

3 Cover the chicken quarters with the spice mixture and leave to marinate for about 3 hours.

4 Preheat the oven to 240°C/475°F/ Gas 9. Transfer the chicken pieces to an ovenproof dish.

5 Bake in the preheated oven for 20–25 minutes, or until the chicken is cooked right through and browned on top.

6 Remove from the oven, transfer to a serving dish and garnish with the salad leaves, lime and tomato.

COOK'S TIP

The red food colouring gives this dish its traditional appearance, but it can be omitted if wished.

Spicy Masala Chicken

These chicken pieces are grilled and have a sweet-and-sour taste. They can be served cold with a salad and rice, or hot with Masala Mashed Potatoes.

INGREDIENTS

Serves 6
12 chicken thighs
90ml/6 tbsp lemon juice
5ml/1 tsp ginger pulp
5ml/1 tsp garlic pulp
5ml/1 tsp crushed dried red chillies
5ml/1 tsp salt
5ml/1 tsp soft brown sugar
30ml/2 tbsp clear honey
30ml/2 tbsp chopped fresh coriander
1 fresh green chilli, finely chopped
30ml/2 tbsp vegetable oil
fresh coriander sprigs, to garnish

COOK'S TIP

Masala refers to the blend of spices used in this dish. The amounts can be varied according to taste.

1 Prick all the chicken thighs with a fork. Rinse them, pat dry and set aside in a bowl.

2 In a large mixing bowl, mix together the lemon juice, ginger, garlic, crushed dried red chillies, salt, sugar and honey.

3 Transfer the chicken thighs to the spice mixture and coat well. Set aside for about 45 minutes.

4 Preheat the grill to medium. Add the fresh coriander and chopped green chilli to the chicken thighs and place them in a flameproof dish.

5 Pour any remaining marinade over the chicken and baste with the oil, using a pastry brush.

6 Grill the chicken thighs under the preheated grill for 15–20 minutes, turning and basting occasionally, until cooked through and browned.

7 Transfer to a serving dish and garnish with the fresh coriander sprigs.

Crispy and Aromatic Duck

As this dish is often served with pancakes, spring onions, cucumber and duck sauce (a sweet bean paste), many people mistake it for Peking Duck. This recipe, however, uses a different cooking method. The result is just as crispy but the delightful aroma makes this dish particularly distinctive. Plum sauce may be substituted for the duck sauce.

INGREDIENTS

Serves 6–8
1 oven-ready duckling,
   about 2.25kg/5–5¼lb
10ml/2 tsp salt
5–6 whole star anise
15ml/1 tbsp Szechuan peppercorns
5ml/1 tsp cloves
2–3 cinnamon sticks
3–4 spring onions
3–4 slices fresh root ginger, unpeeled
75–90ml/5–6 tbsp Chinese rice wine
   or dry sherry
vegetable oil, for deep-frying
lettuce leaves, to garnish

To serve
Chinese pancakes
duck sauce
spring onions, shredded
cucumber, diced

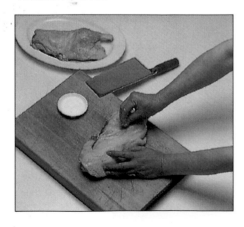

1 Remove the wings from the duck and split the body in half down the backbone.

2 Rub salt all over the two duck halves, taking care to work it all in thoroughly.

3 Marinate the duck in a dish with the spices, spring onions, fresh ginger and wine or sherry for at least 4–6 hours.

4 Vigorously steam the duck with the marinade for 3–4 hours (or for longer if possible). Carefully remove the steamed duck from the cooking liquid and leave to cool for at least 5–6 hours. The duck must be cold and dry or the skin will not be crisp.

5 Heat the vegetable oil in a wok until it is just smoking, then place the duck pieces in the oil, skin-side down. Deep fry the duck for about 5–6 minutes, or until it becomes crisp and brown. Turn the duck just once at the very last moment.

6 Remove the fried duck, drain it well and place it on a bed of lettuce leaves.

7 To serve, scrape the meat off the bone and wrap a portion in each pancake with a little duck sauce, shredded spring onions and cucumber. Eat with your fingers.

COOK'S TIP

Small pancakes suitable for this dish can be found in most Chinese supermarkets. They can be frozen and will keep for up to 3 months in the freezer.

VEGETABLE &
VEGETARIAN
DISHES

~

Red Bean Chilli

This vegetarian chilli can be adapted to accommodate meat eaters by adding either minced beef or lamb in place of the lentils. Add the meat once the onions are soft and fry until nicely browned before adding the tomatoes.

INGREDIENTS

Serves 4

30ml/2 tbsp vegetable oil
1 onion, chopped
400g/14oz can chopped tomatoes
2 garlic cloves, crushed
300ml/½ pint/1¼ cups white wine
about 300ml/½ pint/1¼ cups
    vegetable stock
115g/4oz red lentils
2 thyme sprigs or 5ml/1 tsp dried
    thyme
10ml/2 tsp ground cumin
45ml/3 tbsp dark soy sauce
½ hot chilli pepper, finely chopped
5ml/1 tsp mixed spice
15ml/1 tbsp oyster sauce (optional)
225g/8oz can red kidney beans,
    drained
10ml/2 tsp sugar
salt

1 Heat the oil in a large saucepan and fry the onion over a moderate heat for a few minutes until slightly softened.

2 Add the tomatoes and garlic, cook for 10 minutes, then stir in the wine and stock.

3 Add the lentils, thyme, cumin, soy sauce, hot pepper, mixed spice and oyster sauce, if using.

4 Cover and simmer for 40 minutes or until the lentils are cooked, stirring occasionally and adding more water if the lentils begin to dry out.

5 Stir in the kidney beans and sugar and continue cooking for 10 minutes, adding a little extra stock or water if necessary. Season to taste with salt and serve hot with boiled rice and sweetcorn.

--- COOK'S TIP ---

Fiery chillies can irritate the skin, so always wash your hands well after handling them and take care not to touch your eyes. If you like really hot, spicy food, then add the seeds from the chilli, too.

Spicy Carrots

Adding spices to the carrots before leaving them to cool infuses them with flavour – an ideal dish to serve cold the next day (or up to a week later, if you keep them in the fridge).

INGREDIENTS

Serves 4
450g/1lb carrots
475ml/16fl oz/2 cups water
2.5ml/½ tsp salt
5ml/1 tsp cumin seeds
½–1 red chilli (to taste)
1 large garlic clove, crushed
30ml/2 tbsp olive oil
5ml/1 tsp paprika
juice of 1 lemon
flat leaf parsley, to garnish

1 Cut the carrots into slices about 5mm/¼in thick. Bring the water to the boil and add the salt and carrot slices. Simmer for about 8 minutes or until the carrots are just tender, without allowing them to get too soft. Drain the carrots, put them into a bowl and set aside.

2 Grind or crush the cumin to a powder. Remove the seeds from the chilli and chop the chilli finely. Take care when handling as they can irritate the skin and eyes.

3 Gently heat the oil in a pan and toss in the garlic and the chilli. Stir over medium heat for about a minute, without allowing the garlic to brown. Stir in the paprika and the lemon juice.

4 Pour the warm mixture over the carrots, tossing them well so they are coated with the spices. Spoon into a serving dish and garnish with a sprig of flat leaf parsley.

Kenyan Mung Bean Stew

The Kenyan name for this simple and tasty stew is *Dengu*.

INGREDIENTS

Serves 4

225g/8oz/1¼ cups mung beans, soaked
   overnight
25g/1oz/2 tbsp ghee or butter
2 garlic cloves, crushed
1 red onion, chopped
30ml/2 tbsp tomato purée
½ green pepper, seeded and cut into
   small cubes
½ red pepper, seeded and cut into
   small cubes
1 green chilli, seeded and finely chopped
300ml/½ pint/1¼ cups water

1 Put the mung beans in a large saucepan, cover with water and boil until the beans are soft and the water has evaporated. Remove from the heat and mash roughly with a fork or potato masher.

2 Heat the ghee or butter in a separate saucepan, add the garlic and onion and fry for 4–5 minutes until golden brown, then add the tomato purée and cook for a further 2–3 minutes, stirring all the time.

3 Stir in the mashed beans, then the green and red peppers and chilli.

4 Add the water, stirring well to mix all the ingredients together.

5 Pour back into a clean saucepan and simmer for about 10 minutes, then spoon into a serving dish and serve at once.

— COOK'S TIP —

If you prefer a more traditional, smoother texture, cook the mung beans until very soft, then mash them thoroughly until smooth.

Green Chilli Dhal

This dhal (Tarka Dhal) is probably the most popular of lentil dishes and is found in most Indian and Pakistani restaurants.

INGREDIENTS

Serves 4

115g/4oz/½ cup masoor dhal (split red lentils)
50g/2oz/¼ cup moong dhal (small split yellow lentils)
600ml/1 pint/2½ cups water
5ml/1 tsp ginger pulp
5ml/1 tsp garlic pulp
1.5ml/¼ tsp turmeric
2 fresh green chillies, chopped
7.5ml/1½ tsp salt

For the tarka

30ml/2 tbsp oil
1 onion, sliced
1.5ml/¼ tsp mixed mustard and onion seeds
4 dried red chillies
1 tomato, sliced

To garnish

15ml/1 tbsp chopped fresh coriander
1–2 fresh green chillies, seeded and sliced
15ml/1 tbsp chopped fresh mint

1 Pick over the lentils for any stones before washing them.

2 Boil the lentils in the water with the ginger, garlic, turmeric and chopped green chillies for about 15–20 minutes until soft.

3 Mash the lentil mixture down. The consistency of the mashed lentils should be similar to that of a creamy chicken soup.

4 If the mixture looks too dry, just add some more water. Season with the salt.

5 To prepare the tarka, heat the oil and fry the onion with the mustard and onion seeds, dried red chillies and sliced tomato for 2 minutes.

6 Pour the tarka over the dhal and garnish with fresh coriander, green chillies and mint.

--- COOK'S TIP ---

Dried red chillies are available in many different sizes. If the ones you have are large, or if you want a less spicy flavour, reduce the quantity specified to 1–2.

Frijoles

INGREDIENTS

Serves 6–8

350g/12oz/1¼–1½ cups dried red
  kidney, pinto or black haricot beans,
  picked over and rinsed
2 onions, finely chopped
2 garlic cloves, chopped
1 bay leaf
1 or more *serrano* chillies (small fresh
  green chillies)
30ml/2 tbsp corn oil
2 tomatoes, peeled, seeded and
  chopped
salt
sprigs of fresh bay leaves, to garnish

COOK'S TIP

In Yucatan black haricot beans are cooked
with the Mexican herb *epazote*.

---

1 Put the beans into a pan and add
cold water to cover by 2.5cm/1in.

2 Add half the onion, half the garlic,
the bay leaf and the chilli(es). Bring
to the boil and boil vigorously for
about 10 minutes. Put the beans and
liquid into an earthenware pot or large
saucepan, cover and cook over a low
heat for 30 minutes. Add boiling water
if the mixture starts to become dry.

3 When the beans begin to wrinkle,
add 15ml/1 tbsp of the corn oil
and cook for a further 30 minutes or
until the beans are tender. Add salt to
taste and cook for 30 minutes more,
but do not add any more water.

4 Remove the beans from the heat.
Heat the remaining oil in a small
frying pan and sauté the remaining
onion and garlic until the onion is soft.
Add the tomatoes and cook for a few
minutes more.

5 Spoon 45ml/3 tbsp of the beans
out of the pot or pan and add
them to the tomato mixture. Mash to a
paste. Stir this into the beans to thicken
the liquid. Cook for just long enough
to heat through, if necessary. Serve the
beans in small bowls and garnish with
sprigs of fresh bay leaves.

Broad Bean and Cauliflower Curry

This is a hot and spicy vegetable curry, ideal when served with cooked rice (especially a brown basmati variety), small poppadums and maybe a cooling cucumber raita as well.

INGREDIENTS

Serves 4
2 garlic cloves, chopped
2.5cm/1in cube fresh root ginger
1 fresh green chilli, seeded
  and chopped
15ml/1 tbsp oil
1 onion, sliced
1 large potato, chopped
30ml/2 tbsp ghee or softened butter
15ml/1 tbsp curry powder, mild or hot
1 cauliflower, cut into small florets
600ml/1 pint/2½ cups stock
30ml/2 tbsp creamed coconut
275g/10oz can broad beans, and liquor
juice of ½ lemon (optional)
salt and ground black pepper
fresh coriander, chopped, to garnish

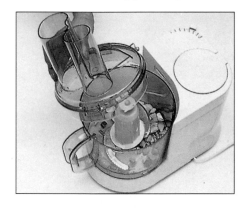

1 Blend the garlic, ginger, chilli and oil in a food processor or blender until they form a smooth paste.

2 In a large saucepan, fry the onion and potato in the ghee or butter for 5 minutes, then stir in the spice paste and curry powder. Cook for 1 minute.

3 Add the cauliflower florets and stir well into the spicy mixture, then pour in the stock. Bring to the boil and mix in the creamed coconut, stirring until it melts.

4 Season well, then cover and simmer for 10 minutes. Add the beans and their liquor and cook, uncovered, for a further 10 minutes.

5 Check the seasoning and add a good squeeze of lemon juice, if liked. Serve hot, garnished with the chopped coriander.

Masala Mashed Potatoes

These potatoes are very versatile
and will perk up any meal.

INGREDIENTS

Serves 4
3 potatoes
15ml/1 tbsp chopped fresh mint
   and coriander, mixed
5ml/1 tsp mango powder
5ml/1 tsp salt
5ml/1 tsp crushed black peppercorns
1 fresh red chilli, chopped
1 fresh green chilli, chopped
50g/2oz/4 tbsp margarine

1 Boil the potatoes until soft enough
to be mashed. Mash them down
using a masher.

2 Blend together the chopped herbs,
mango powder, salt, pepper,
chillies and margarine to form a paste.

3 Stir the mixture into the mashed
potatoes and mix together
thoroughly with a fork. Serve warm as
an accompaniment.

VARIATION

Instead of potatoes, try sweet potatoes.
Cook them until tender, mash and continue from step 2.

Spicy Cabbage

An excellent vegetable
accompaniment, this is a very
versatile spicy dish that can also
be served as a warm side salad.
It's so quick to make that it can
be a handy last minute addition
to any meal.

INGREDIENTS

Serves 4
50g/2oz/4 tbsp margarine
2.5ml/½ tsp white cumin seeds
3–8 dried red chillies, to taste
1 small onion, sliced
225g/8oz/2½ cups cabbage, shredded
2 carrots, grated
2.5ml/½ tsp salt
30ml/2 tbsp lemon juice

1 Melt the margarine in a saucepan
and fry the white cumin seeds and
dried red chillies for about
30 seconds.

2 Add the sliced onion and fry for
about 2 minutes. Add the cabbage
and carrots and stir-fry for a further
5 minutes until the cabbage is soft.

3 Finally, stir in the salt and lemon
juice and serve.

Vegetables in Peanut and Chilli Sauce

INGREDIENTS

Serves 4

15ml/1 tbsp palm or vegetable oil
1 onion, chopped
2 garlic cloves, crushed
400g/14oz can tomatoes, puréed
45ml/3 tbsp smooth peanut butter,
    preferably unsalted
750ml/1¼ pint/3⅔ cups water
5ml/1 tsp dried thyme
1 green chilli, seeded and chopped
1 vegetable stock cube
2.5ml/½ tsp ground allspice
2 carrots
115g/4oz white cabbage
175g/6oz okra
½ red pepper
150ml/¼ pint/⅔ cup vegetable stock
salt

1 Heat the oil in a large saucepan and fry the onion and garlic over a moderate heat for 5 minutes, stirring frequently. Add the tomatoes and peanut butter and stir well.

2 Stir in the water, thyme, chilli, stock cube, allspice and a little salt. Bring to the boil and then simmer gently, uncovered for about 35 minutes.

3 Cut the carrots into sticks, slice the cabbage, top and tail the okra and seed and slice the red pepper.

4 Place the vegetables in a saucepan with the stock, bring to the boil and cook until tender but still with a little "bite".

5 Drain the vegetables and place in a warmed serving dish. Pour the sauce over the top and serve.

Marinated Vegetables on Skewers

These kebabs are a delightful main dish for vegetarians, or serve them as a vegetable side dish.

INGREDIENTS

Serves 4
115g/4oz pumpkin
1 red onion
1 small courgette
1 ripe plantain
1 aubergine
1/2 red pepper, seeded
1/2 green pepper, seeded
12 button mushrooms
60ml/4 tbsp lemon juice
60ml/4 tbsp olive or sunflower oil
45–60ml/3–4 tbsp soy sauce
150ml/1/4 pint/2/3 cup tomato juice
1 green chilli, seeded and chopped
1/2 onion, grated
3 garlic cloves, crushed
7.5ml/1 1/2 tsp dried tarragon, crushed
4ml/3/4 tsp dried basil
4ml/3/4 tsp dried thyme
4ml/3/4 tsp ground cinnamon
25g/1oz/2 tbsp butter or margarine
300ml/1/2 pint/1 1/4 cups vegetable stock
freshly ground black pepper
fresh parsley sprigs, to garnish

1 Peel and cube the pumpkin, place in a small bowl and cover with boiling water. Blanch for 2–3 minutes, then drain and refresh under cold water.

2 Cut the onion into wedges, slice the courgette and plantain and cut the aubergine and red and green peppers into chunks. Trim the mushrooms. Place the vegetables, including the pumpkin in a large bowl.

3 Mix together the lemon juice, oil, soy sauce, tomato juice, chili, grated onion, garlic, herbs, cinnamon and black pepper and pour over the vegetables. Toss together and then set aside in a cool place to marinate for a few hours.

4 Thread the vegetables on to eight skewers, using a variety of vegetables on each to make a colourful display. Preheat the grill.

5 Grill the vegetables under a low heat, for about 15 minutes, turning frequently, until golden brown, basting with the marinade to keep the vegetables moist.

6 Place the remaining marinade, butter or margarine and stock in a pan and simmer for 10 minutes to cook the onion and reduce the sauce.

7 Pour the sauce into a serving jug and arrange the vegetable skewers on a plate. Garnish with parsley and serve with a rice dish or salad.

--- COOK'S TIP ---

You can use any vegetable that you prefer. Just first parboil any that may require longer cooking.

Spicy Vegetables with Almonds

INGREDIENTS

Serves 4

30ml/2 tbsp vegetable oil
2 onions, sliced
5cm/2in fresh root ginger, shredded
5ml/1 tsp crushed black peppercorns
1 bay leaf
1.5ml/¼ tsp turmeric
5ml/1 tsp ground coriander
5ml/1 tsp salt
2.5ml/½ tsp garam masala
175g/6oz/2½ cups mushrooms, sliced
1 courgette, thickly sliced
50g/2oz French beans, sliced into
  2.5cm/1in pieces
15ml/1 tbsp chopped fresh mint
150ml/¼ pint/⅔ cup water
30ml/2 tbsp natural low-fat yogurt
25g/1oz/¼ cup flaked almonds

1 In a medium deep frying pan, heat the vegetable oil and fry the sliced onions with the shredded fresh ginger, crushed black peppercorns and the bay leaf for 3–5 minutes.

2 Lower the heat and add the turmeric, ground coriander, salt and garam masala, stirring occasionally. Gradually add the mushrooms, courgette, French beans and the mint. Stir gently so that the vegetables retain their shape.

3 Pour in the water and bring to a simmer, then lower the heat and cook until most of the water has evaporated.

4 Beat the natural low-fat yogurt well with a fork, then pour it on to the vegetables in the pan and mix together well.

5 Cook the spicy vegetables for a further 2–3 minutes, stirring occasionally. Sprinkle with flaked almonds and serve.

— COOK'S TIP —

For an extra creamy dish, add soured cream instead of the natural yogurt.

Masala Beans with Fenugreek

"Masala" means spice and this vegetarian dish is spicy, though not necessarily hot. You can adapt the spiciness of the dish by using smaller or larger quantities of the spices, as you wish. Serve it as an accompaniment to a meat dish with freshly cooked basmati rice for a wonderful Indian meal.

INGREDIENTS

Serves 4
1 onion
5ml/1 tsp ground cumin
5ml/1 tsp ground coriander
5ml/1 tsp sesame seeds
5ml/1 tsp chilli powder
2.5ml/½ tsp garlic pulp
1.5ml/¼ tsp turmeric
5ml/1 tsp salt
30ml/2 tbsp vegetable oil
1 tomato, quartered
225g/8oz French beans
1 bunch fresh fenugreek leaves,
   stems discarded
60ml/4 tbsp chopped fresh coriander
15ml/1 tbsp lemon juice

1 Roughly chop the onion. In a mixing bowl, combine the ground cumin and coriander, sesame seeds, chilli powder, garlic pulp, turmeric and salt. Mix well.

2 Place all of these ingredients, including the onion, in a food processor or blender and process for 30–45 seconds.

3 In a medium saucepan, heat the vegetable oil and fry the spice mixture for about 5 minutes, stirring it occasionally as it cooks.

4 Add the quartered tomato, French beans, fresh fenugreek and fresh chopped coriander.

5 Stir-fry the mixture for about 5 minutes, then sprinkle over the lemon juice, pour into a serving dish and serve immediately.

COOK'S TIP

If you can't find fenugreek leaves, use 5ml/1 tsp fenugreek seeds instead.

Balti Potatoes

Balti is a traditional way of cooking Indian curries in a karahi cooking pan.

INGREDIENTS

Serves 4

75ml/3 tbsp corn oil
2.5ml/½ tsp white cumin seeds
3 curry leaves
5ml/1 tsp crushed dried red chillies
2.5ml/½ tsp mixed onion, mustard and fenugreek seeds
2.5ml/½ tsp fennel seeds
3 garlic cloves
2.5ml/½ tsp shredded ginger
2 onions, sliced
6 new potatoes, sliced thinly
15ml/1 tbsp chopped fresh coriander
1 fresh red chilli, seeded and sliced
1 fresh green chilli, seeded and sliced

1 Heat the oil in a deep round-bottomed frying pan or a karahi. Lower the heat slightly and add the cumin seeds, curry leaves, dried red chillies, mixed onion, mustard and fenugreek seeds, fennel seeds, garlic cloves and ginger. Fry for 1 minute, then add the onions and fry for a further 5 minutes, or until the onions are golden brown.

2 Add the potatoes, fresh coriander and fresh red and green chillies and mix well. Cover the pan tightly with a lid or foil, making sure the foil does not touch the food. Cook over a very low heat for about 7 minutes, or until the potatoes are tender.

3 Remove the pan from the heat, take off the foil and serve hot.

Okra with Green Mango and Lentils

If you like okra, you'll love this spicy tangy dish.

INGREDIENTS

Serves 4

115g/4oz/½ cup yellow lentils (toor dhal)
45ml/3 tbsp corn oil
2.5ml/½ tsp onion seeds
2 onions, sliced
2.5ml/½ tsp ground fenugreek
5ml/1 tsp ginger pulp
5ml/1 tsp garlic pulp
7.5ml/1½ tsp chilli powder
1.5ml/¼ tsp turmeric
5ml/1 tsp ground coriander
1 green mango, peeled and sliced
450g/1lb okra, cut into 1cm/½in pieces
7.5ml/1½ tsp salt
2 fresh red chillies, seeded and sliced
30ml/2 tbsp chopped fresh coriander
1 tomato, sliced

1 Wash the lentils thoroughly and put in a saucepan with enough water to cover. Bring to the boil and cook until soft but not mushy. Drain and set to one side.

2 Heat the oil in a deep round-bottomed frying pan or a karahi and fry the onion seeds until they begin to pop. Add the onions and fry until golden brown. Lower the heat and add the ground fenugreek, ginger, garlic, chilli powder, turmeric and ground coriander.

3 Throw in the mango slices and the okra. Stir well and add the salt, red chillies and fresh coriander. Stir-fry for about 3 minutes, or until the okra is well cooked.

4 Finally, add the cooked lentils and sliced tomato and cook for a further 3 minutes. Serve hot.

RELISHES

Salsa Verde

There are many versions of this classic green salsa. Serve this one with creamy mashed potatoes or drizzled over the top of char-grilled squid.

INGREDIENTS

Serves 4
2–4 green chillies
8 spring onions
2 garlic cloves
50g/2oz salted capers
fresh tarragon sprig
1 bunch of fresh parsley
grated rind and juice of 1 lime
juice of 1 lemon
90ml/6 tbsp olive oil
about 15ml/1 tbsp green Tabasco, or
   to taste
ground black pepper

1 Halve the green chillies and remove their seeds. Trim the spring onions and halve the garlic, then place in a food processor or blender. Pulse the power briefly until the ingredients are roughly chopped.

2 Use your fingertips to rub the excess salt off the capers but do not rinse them. Add the capers, tarragon and parsley to the food processor or blender and pulse again until they are fairly finely chopped.

3 Transfer the mixture to a small bowl. Stir in the lime rind and juice, lemon juice and olive oil. Stir the mixture lightly so the citrus juice and oil do not emulsify.

4 Add green Tabasco and black pepper to taste. Chill until ready to serve but do not prepare more than 8 hours in advance.

VARIATION

If you can find only capers pickled in vinegar, they can be used for this salsa but they must be rinsed well in cold water first.

Fiery Citrus Salsa

This very unusual salsa makes a fantastic marinade for all kinds of shellfish and it is also delicious when drizzled over freshly barbecued meat.

INGREDIENTS

Serves 4

1 orange
1 green apple
2 fresh red chillies, halved and seeded
1 garlic clove
8 fresh mint leaves
juice of 1 lemon
salt and ground black pepper

1 Slice the bottom off the orange so that it stands firmly on a chopping board. Using a large sharp knife, remove the peel by slicing from the top to the bottom of the orange.

2 Hold the orange in one hand over a bowl. Slice towards the middle of the fruit, to one side of a segment, and then gently twist the knife to ease the segment away from the membrane and out of the orange. Repeat to remove all the segments. Squeeze any juice from the remaining membrane.

3 Peel the apple, slice it into wedges and remove the core.

4 Place the chillies in a blender or food processor with the orange segments and juice, apple wedges, garlic and mint.

5 Process until smooth, then, with the motor running, pour in the lemon juice.

6 Season, pour into a bowl or small jug and serve immediately.

VARIATION

If you're feeling really fiery, don't seed the chillies! They will make the salsa particularly hot and fierce.

Piquant Pineapple Relish

This fruity sweet and sour relish is really excellent when it is served with grilled chicken or bacon rashers.

INGREDIENTS

Serves 4

400g/14oz can crushed pineapple in
    natural juice
30ml/2 tbsp light muscovado sugar
30ml/2 tbsp wine vinegar
1 garlic clove
4 spring onions
2 red chillies
10 fresh basil leaves
salt and ground black pepper

1 Drain the crushed pineapple pieces thoroughly and reserve about 60ml/4 tbsp of the juice.

2 Place the juice in a small saucepan with the muscovado sugar and wine vinegar, then heat gently, stirring, until the sugar dissolves. Remove the pan from the heat and add salt and pepper to taste.

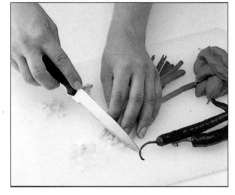

3 Finely chop the garlic and spring onions. Halve the chillies, remove the seeds and finely chop them. Finely shred the basil.

4 Place the pineapple, garlic, spring onions and chillies in a bowl. Mix well and pour in the sauce. Allow to cool for 5 minutes, then stir in the basil.

COOK'S TIP

This relish tastes extra special when made with fresh pineapple – substitute the juice of a freshly squeezed orange for the canned juice.

Mixed Vegetable Pickle

If you can obtain fresh turmeric, it makes such a difference to the colour and appearance of *Acar Campur*. You can use almost any vegetable, bearing in mind that you need a balance of textures, flavours and colours.

INGREDIENTS

Makes 2–3 x 300g/11oz jars
1 fresh red chilli, seeded and sliced
1 onion, quartered
2 garlic cloves, crushed
1cm/½ in cube *terasi*
4 macadamia nuts or 8 almonds
2.5cm/1in fresh turmeric, peeled and
   sliced, or 5ml/1 tsp ground turmeric
50ml/2fl oz/¼ cup sunflower oil
475ml/16fl oz/2 cups white vinegar
250ml/8fl oz/1 cup water
25–50g/1–2oz granulated sugar
3 carrots
225g/8oz green beans
1 small cauliflower
1 cucumber
225g/8oz white cabbage
115g/4oz dry-roasted peanuts,
   roughly crushed
salt

1 Place the chilli, onion, garlic, *terasi*, nuts and turmeric in a food processor and blend to a paste, or pound in a mortar with a pestle.

2 Heat the oil and stir-fry the paste to release the aroma. Add the vinegar, water, sugar and salt. Bring to the boil. Simmer for 10 minutes.

3 Cut the carrots into flower shapes. Cut the green beans into short, neat lengths. Separate the cauliflower into neat, bite-size florets. Peel and seed the cucumber and cut the flesh in neat, bite-size pieces. Cut the cabbage in neat, bite-size pieces.

4 Blanch each vegetable separately, in a large pan of boiling water, for 1 minute. Transfer to a colander and rinse with cold water, to halt the cooking. Drain well.

> — COOK'S TIP —
>
> This pickle is even better if you make it a few days ahead.

5 Add the vegetables to the sauce. Slowly bring to the boil and allow to cook for 5–10 minutes. Do not overcook – the vegetables should still be crunchy.

6 Add the peanuts and cool. Spoon into clean jars with lids.

Red Onion Raita

Raita is a traditional Indian accompaniment for most hot curries. It is also delicious when served with a pile of spicy poppadums as a dip.

INGREDIENTS

Serves 4

5ml/1 tsp cumin seeds
1 small garlic clove
1 small green chilli, seeded
1 large red onion
150ml/¼ pint/⅔ cup natural yogurt
30ml/2 tbsp chopped fresh coriander, plus extra to garnish
2.5ml/½ tsp sugar
salt

1 Heat a small frying pan and dry fry the cumin seeds for 1–2 minutes, until they release their aroma and begin to pop.

2 Lightly crush the cumin seeds in a pestle and mortar, or flatten them with the heel of a heavy-bladed knife until crushed.

3 Finely chop the garlic, green chilli and red onion. Stir into the yogurt with the crushed cumin seeds and chopped coriander.

4 Add sugar and salt to taste. Spoon the raita into a small bowl and chill until ready to serve. Garnish with extra coriander before serving.

─── COOK'S TIP ───

For an extra tangy raita, stir in 15ml/1 tbsp lemon juice.

Kachumbali Salad

Katchumbali is a peppery relish from Tanzania, where it is served with grilled meat or fish dishes, together with rice – this salad uses the same combination of vegetables and flavours.

INGREDIENTS

Serves 4–6
2 red onions
4 tomatoes
1 green chilli
½ cucumber
1 carrot
juice of 1 lemon
salt and freshly ground black pepper

1 Slice the onions and tomatoes very thinly and place in a bowl.

2 Slice the chilli lengthways, discard the seeds, then chop very finely. Peel and slice the cucumber and carrot and add to the onions and tomatoes.

3 Squeeze the lemon juice over the salad. Season with salt and freshly ground black pepper and toss together to mix. Serve as an accompaniment, salad or relish.

COOK'S TIP

Traditional *Katchumbali* is made by very finely chopping the onions, tomatoes, cucumber and carrot. This produces a very moist, sauce-like mixture, which is good served inside chapatis, and eaten as a snack.

Coconut Chilli Relish

This simple but delicious relish is widely made in Tanzania. Only the white part of the coconut flesh is used – either shred it fairly coarsely, or grate it finely for a moister result.

INGREDIENTS

Makes about 50g/2oz
50g/2oz fresh or desiccated coconut
10ml/2 tsp lemon juice
1.5ml/¼ tsp salt
10ml/2 tsp water
1.5ml/¼ tsp finely chopped red chilli

1 Grate the coconut and place in a mixing bowl. If using desiccated coconut, add just enough water to moisten.

2 Add the lemon juice, salt, water and chilli. Stir thoroughly and serve as a relish with meats or as an accompaniment to a main dish.

Chilli Bean Dip

This creamy and spicy dip made from kidney beans is best served warm with triangles of golden brown grilled pitta bread or a generous helping of crunchy tortilla chips.

INGREDIENTS

Serves 4

2 garlic cloves
1 onion
2 fresh green chillies
30ml/2 tbsp vegetable oil
5–10ml/1–2 tsp hot chilli powder
400g/14oz can kidney beans
75g/3oz mature Cheddar
  cheese, grated
1 red chilli, seeded
salt and ground black pepper

1 Finely chop the garlic and onion. Seed and finely chop the fresh green chillies.

2 Heat the oil in a frying pan and add the garlic, onion, green chillies and chilli powder. Cook gently for 5 minutes, stirring regularly, until the onions are softened.

3 Drain the can of kidney beans, reserving the liquor. Blend all but 30ml/2 tbsp of the beans to a purée in a food processor or blender.

4 Add the puréed beans to the pan with 30–45ml/2–3 tbsp of the reserved liquor. Heat gently, stirring to mix well.

5 Stir in the whole kidney beans and the grated Cheddar cheese. Cook gently for about 2–3 minutes, stirring until all the cheese melts. Add salt and plenty of freshly ground black pepper to taste.

6 Cut the fresh red chilli into tiny strips. Spoon the dip into four individual serving bowls and scatter the chilli strips over the top of each one. Serve warm.

COOK'S TIP

For a dip with a coarser texture, do not purée the kidney beans in a food processor or blender; instead, mash them with a potato masher.

Chilli Relish

This spicy tomato and red pepper relish will keep for at least a week in the fridge. Serve it with bangers and burgers in fresh white baps with a crisp salad.

INGREDIENTS

Serves 8

6 tomatoes
1 onion
1 red pepper, seeded
2 garlic cloves
30ml/2 tbsp olive oil
5ml/1 tsp ground cinnamon
5ml/1 tsp chilli flakes
5ml/1 tsp ground ginger
5ml/1 tsp salt
2.5ml/½ tsp ground black pepper
75g/3oz/⅓ cup light muscovado sugar
75ml/5 tbsp cider vinegar
1 handful of fresh basil leaves

COOK'S TIP

This relish thickens slightly on cooling so don't worry if the mixture seems a little wet at the end of step 5.

1 Skewer each of the tomatoes in turn on a metal fork and hold in a gas flame for 1–2 minutes, turning until the skin splits and wrinkles. Slip off the skins, then roughly chop the tomatoes.

2 Roughly chop the onion, red pepper and garlic. Heat the oil in a saucepan. Add the onion, red pepper and garlic.

3 Cook gently for 5–8 minutes, until the pepper is softened. Add the chopped tomatoes, cover and cook for 5 minutes, until the tomatoes release their juices.

4 Stir in the cinnamon, chilli flakes, ginger, salt, pepper, sugar and vinegar. Bring gently to the boil, stirring until the sugar dissolves.

5 Simmer, uncovered, for about 20 minutes, or until the mixture is pulpy. Stir in the basil leaves and check the seasoning.

6 Allow the relish to cool completely, then transfer it to a glass jam jar or a plastic container with a tightly fitting lid. Store, covered, in the fridge.

INDEX